I0018202

Java for Small Teams - Guidance for good server side code

A catalogue record for this book is available from the Hong Kong Public Libraries.

Published in Hong Kong by Samurai Media Limited.

Email: info@samuraimedia.org

ISBN 978-988-8407-21-7

Background Cover Image by https://www.flickr.com/people/webtreatsetc/

Table of Contents

Introduction

What is This?

This book is an attempt to capture what *"good"* Java code looks like and the practices that help produce it.

This is a problematic document to write.

There is no one right answer to what good code looks like and there are many well-respected books that serve the same purpose such as *Effective Java*, *Clean Code* and others.

So why this document?

It differentiates itself by being :

- Freely distributable
- Open for update - contributions, corrections and updates are encouraged
- Brief - much is left out in an attempt to be easily digestible
- Narrow - it captures one opinion of *"good"* appropriate for a specific context

This last point is important.

We assume a number of things about you and the environment you are working in.

- We assume you are writing server side Java in *small* teams.
- We assume your teams are of mixed experience (some experts, some beginners).
- We assume you are writing code in a general "business" context.
- We assume you expect the code to still be in use in five years' time.

Some of the suggestions may be valid in other contexts, others might constitute terrible advice for those contexts.

It is also just one opinion from many valid alternatives. To be useful it needs to be an opinion that you can agree with and sign up to. If you disagree with something in this book please make your own thoughts known so it can be improved.

Finally, not all the code we work on is perfect. Sometimes we inherit our own mistakes, sometimes we inherit other people's.

The point of this document is not to say that all code must look like this but to have an agreed destination that we are aiming for.

Who is This For?

This document is intended for consumption by anyone involved with writing server side Java code. From developers writing Java for the first time through to seasoned technical leads serving multiple teams.

Some sections will be more relevant to some audiences than others but we encourage everyone to at least skim all sections even if you do not read them in depth.

Structure

The document is split into five sections:

- Process - Discussion on development philosophy and workflow
- Style - Good style and design at a high level
- Specifics - More specific advice on Java language features and gotchas
- Good tests - How to write good tests
- Bad advice - Discussion of some commonly circulated bad advice and patterns

Version

This book is updated often. The latest changes to the book can be viewed online at gitbook.com.

Versioned releases are available for free from the book's website.

If you are reading a PDF or print copy of this book the release version will be displayed on the inside cover. If there is no inside cover then you are reading an unreleased version of the book.

History

Most of the content of this book began life as internal wiki pages at NCR Edinburgh. We started to convert the wiki into this book at the end of 2015 so that it could be easily shared with other parts of our company.

Rather than keep this as an internal document we decided to open it up to everyone in the hope that together we could make it better.

A word on Trade-Offs

There are no right answers in software engineering.

It is a balancing act in which we must trade off one concern against another and make a judgement call about which balance is better for the specific scenario we have found ourselves in.

One of the most common mistakes we've seen experienced programmers make is to blindly consider only one or two concerns (often the ones with catchy acronyms) without thought for others.

We've carefully set out the context in which we think the advice in this book will be useful, but the context is still very broad. Slightly different situations might benefit from very different trade offs. What worked well for you in one project might not work so well in the next.

For this reason we rarely use words like *always* or *never*.

When we do use them we have thought carefully before doing so, but what we really mean is almost-always or almost-never.

Having said this if you find yourself discounting any of the recommendations in this book please stop and think first. Don't fall into the trap of thinking certain advice cannot apply to you. We often make our worst mistakes when we believe we are being elegant or clever. The full horror of our ineptitude sometimes does not become apparent for months or years.

Advice is here to save us from ourselves.

A note on Java Versions

This document is intended to apply to Java 7 and 8, but will be largely applicable to Java 5 and 6.

Where there are differences between Java 8 and 7 we will point them out. If you are unlucky enough to be working with an earlier version of Java you will have to discover any differences to Java 7 on your own.

License

Author

This document was written by Henry Coles and numerous contributors.

Contributors

- Francesco Burato
- Gary Duprex
- Grant Forrester
- Kevin Grant
- Keir Lawson
- Marco Di Paola
- Gordon Rogers
- Herve Saint-Amand
- Ewan Summers

Cover

The cover was produced by Peter Berry based on a wood engraving of a Long billed curlew from the 1885 text *"Nouveau dictionnaire encyclopédique universel illustré"*

To our knowledge Long Billed Curlews are not especially proficient in Java.

Process

Code (good and bad) doesn't just appear from nowhere, someone needs to sit down and write it. How the coder approaches this task can influence the amount of time spent swearing at the code later.

This section looks at development philosophy, workflow, and other factors that teams should consider before starting to work together.

Build Fast Feedback Loops

Good code is all about getting good and timely feedback. The sooner you find out something is wrong the easier it is to fix.

Working on a legacy project, where the only way to discover if a code change is good is to deploy it to a dev/test/qa environment, is frustrating and demoralizing.

Make sure your project has a well designed development workflow - the effort of setting this up will be repaid many times over.

Ideally all feedback would be instantaneous, but in practice it is either impractical or impossible to get all feedback this way.

Instead software development is organized as nested levels of feedback, as shown here:

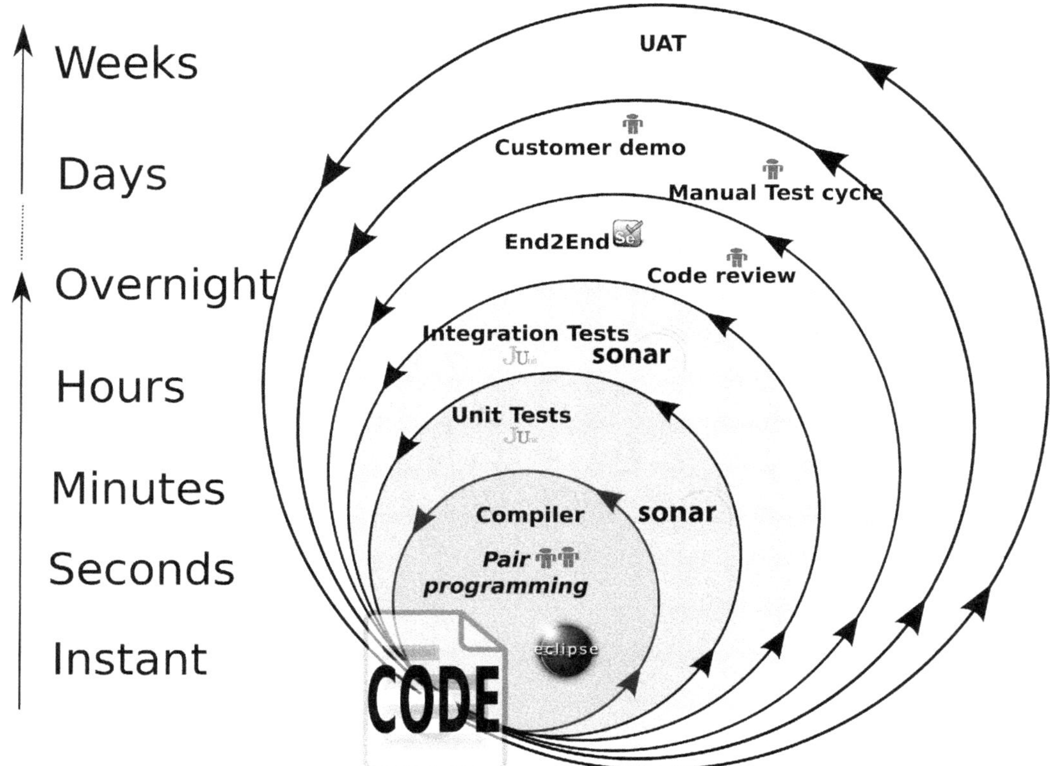

Instant Feedback

A modern IDE such as Eclipse or IntelliJ will provide instant feedback as you type, using the underlying compiler and configurable static analysis tools.

You can increase the amount of instant feedback you receive by making good use of the Java type system and configuring the static analysis tools.

While feedback from the IDE is fast and convenient, it has some drawbacks.

- It may differ from machine to machine depending on the IDE configuration
- It is often non binary (i.e. not pass/fail)
- It can be ignored / overlooked
- The expectation of speed limits what it can achieve

For these reasons you should avoid purely IDE centric work flows. Code should not be considered complete by a developer until tests have been run via the build file.

Fast Feedback

The Build File is Truth

The build script provides less-immediate feedback than the IDE because it must be explicitly triggered.

Feedback from the build script has two major advantages, however:

- It is repeatable across all machines
- With the aid of a CI server, you can ensure it is not ignored

Because slower feedback is acceptable from the build script, a larger set of static and dynamic analysis can be run from here. This will usually include a repeat of your instant feedback.

Locally Runnable Tests

After the compiler and static analysis, the next fastest levels of feedback are the test suites.

At least two suites should be maintained that are runnable locally on any developer machine.

Because they are typically run immediately after compiling or before committing/pushing code, Martin Fowler refers to these as:

- The compile suite
- The commit suite

In Maven, these map naturally to the `test` and `integration-test` phases.

The criteria for a test being placed in the compile suite should, however, be more than **just** its execution speed.

They must be fast (milliseconds or less per test) but must also be highly deterministic and repeatable. This ensures that the suite provides clean feedback - the only reason that a test should fail after a code change is if the change has caused regression.

Although this sounds simple, in practice it requires considerable rigor to ensure that tests cannot interfere with each other or be affected by external factors.

Tests in the commit suite may be slower and may also be slightly less repeatable. They should **aim** to be 100% repeatable but they may do things that carry the risk of occasionally causing a failure, like use network IO or write to disk.

Although many tests in this suite may do no more than launch code within the same JVM as the tests themselves, some of the tests should also launch the built artifact (war, ear, jar) and perform at least some degree of testing against it.

Although the commit suite will likely depend on external resources such as containers, databases, queues, etc., it should still be runnable on any machine with a single command.

Installing and starting dependent resources should be handled automatically by the build scripts and tests - your project should not come with a page of notes on how to set up a development machine.

Commonly, the Maven Cargo plugin is used to download and configure containers for testing.

Slower Feedback

Both the compile suite and the commit suite should be run on a CI server, normally triggered by a commit/push to the repository.

In addition to the compile and commit suites, other suites should be created.

These suites may require resources not available on a local machine and/or take large amounts of time to execute.

They may also re-run the same tests against more realistic dependencies. If an in-memory database is normally used when running integration tests locally, the same tests might be run again against a production database.

For a Maven build, these suites are likely to be implemented using profiles or as separate Maven modules.

These suites will be run as frequently as possible. Most likely, this will mean on a timed basis because it is likely they will consume too much time to be run on commit. Here, "too much time" is defined as taking longer than the likely interval between commits/pushes to the monitored repository.

Timed test runs also sometimes run the suites when no code changes have occurred - this can provide useful information when identifying flaky tests.

Agree the Language You Use When Discussing Tests

The Testing Pyramid

Unfortunately, the language of testing is heavily overloaded, with different communities referring to different things by the same names.

The testing pyramid is a widely recognized diagram of how testing should be approached.

It shows large numbers of unit tests at the bottom, with a smaller number of integration tests above them and a yet smaller number of system tests at the peak. Often, some clouds of manual testing are added at the top.

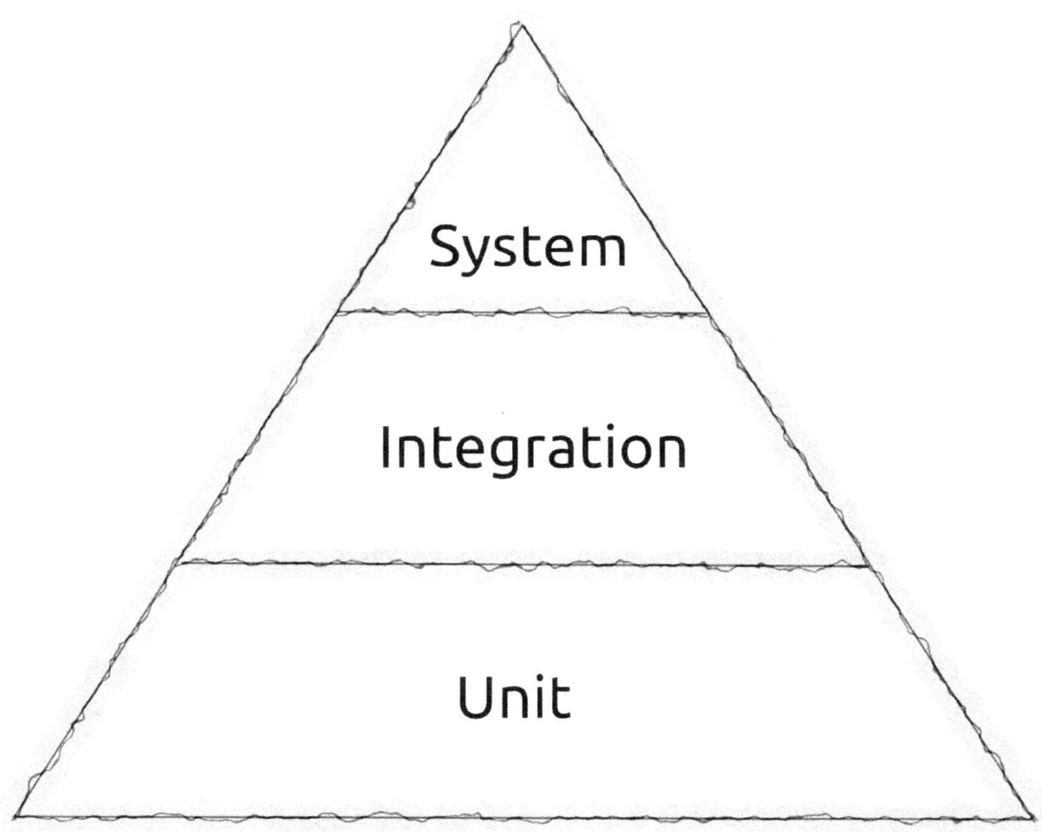

This diagram has probably been drawn thousands of times. Although unit tests will appear at the bottom of each version, the words used at the other levels will vary wildly.

Even when the same words are used the meanings attached to them might be different.

Although people might nod when you discuss "unit tests", "integration tests", "system tests", "end 2 end tests", "service tests", there is no guarantee that they are thinking of the same thing as you.

Depending on who you speak to, a "unit test" might be anything from a word document full of instructions, "any test written by a programmer", through to various formal (but by no means authoritative) definitions that appeared in text books.

The number of possible meanings of "integration test" is even greater.

Unit Tests

A fairly tight definition of unit tests is now in common use in the Java community. We recommend that you and your team use this definition.

To be a unit test, a test must be:

- Fast (milliseconds or less)
- Isolated (test only one unit)
- Repeatable (able to be run millions of times on any machine with the same result)
- Self verifying (either passes or fails)
- Timely (written first)

Note: Although writing your tests first is often a very good idea, a test that meets the other criteria is still a unit test regardless of when it was written.

When we talk about "unit" testing, what constitutes a *unit* isn't necessarily that obvious.

A somewhat circular definition is that a *unit* is the smallest thing that makes sense to test independently.

It will often be a single class, but this is not necessarily the case. It may make sense to treat a group of classes as a unit (particularly if most of them are non-public) or occasionally even a method.

If we accept that a *unit* is a small thing, and that we'll know it when we see it, then we can see that the criteria for being a unit test largely matches the criteria we put forward for the compile suite.

The only difference is that the compile suite does not care about isolation.

If we choose to write a test that tests two (or more) *units* in tandem, it still belongs in the compile suite if it meets the other criteria.

System Tests

System tests are also fairly well-defined. They are tests that exercise the overall system - i.e all your code and all the code it interacts with in a realistic environment.

Integration Tests

Integration tests are harder to define. They occupy the large space of everything that doesn't fit the unit or system tests definitions.

The two following diagrams show how this terminology fits into our world of test suites.

This document will use the terminology *unit test*, *Integration test* and *System test* as shown in these diagrams.

For clarity, it will sometimes state exactly what is being tested when discussing integration tests - e.g "test via the REST API of the war file running in Tomcat".

Although it is tedious, this long-hand terminology is clear. It is recommended that you use it when discussing testing across teams. Within your own team it is likely you will develop a shorter language you all understand.

	Fast and Repeatable **extremely** Deterministic	Self Contained Slow or **Less** deterministic	Environment Dependent
Unit	Unit	Integration	Integration
Component	Unit	Integration	Integration
Artefact		Integration	Integration
System			System

This maps to our suites as shown below:

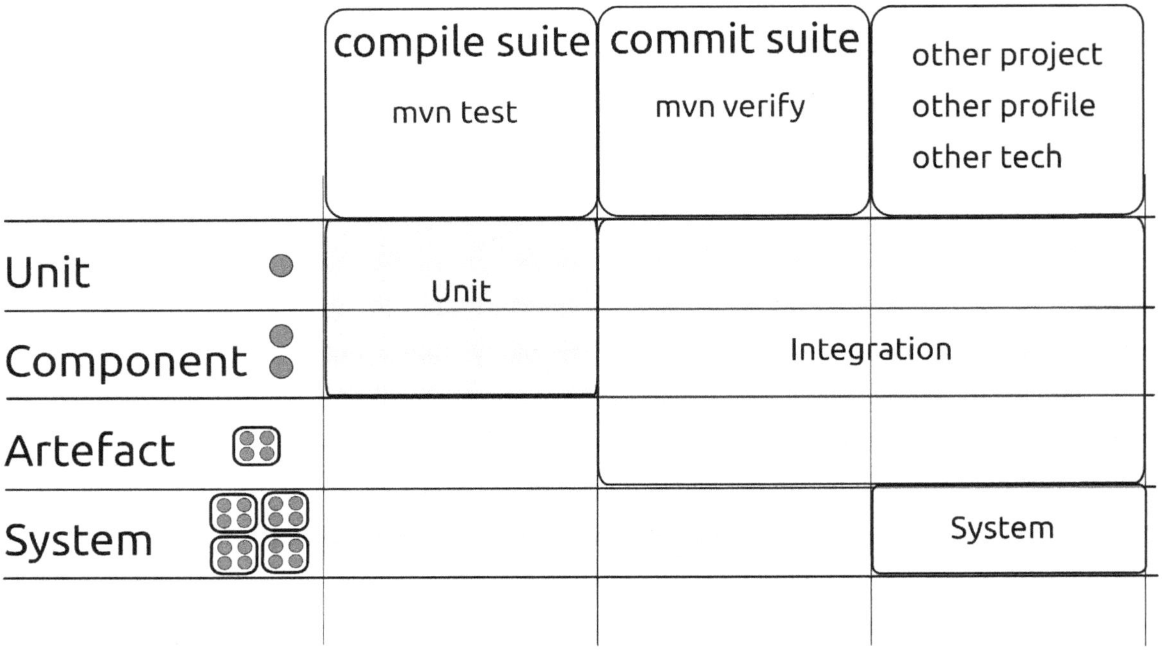

	compile suite mvn test	commit suite mvn verify	other project other profile other tech
Unit	Unit	Integration	
Component			
Artefact			
System			System

Use Coverage as a Tool, not a Target

Code coverage is a useful tool for catching your mistakes.

The tool should work for you; you do not work for the tool.

It is most useful when code coverage is run at the point at which the code and tests are being written, rather than on a CI server hours later.

Gaps in code coverage highlight areas of code that have not been tested. Some of these gaps may be expected and intentional, others may be a surprise. It is these surprise gaps that provide useful information.

This is all that code coverage does.

Code that has 100% branch coverage may or may not have been tested. Code coverage tells you that some tests have executed the code, not that they have meaningfully tested it. Don't let it lull you into a false sense of security.

Some teams set coverage targets that code must meet (75% seems to be a common figure). Although well-intentioned, this practice is often damaging.

Code coverage is easy to measure. Other properties of tests that are desirable (or highly undesirable) are not easy to measure e.g.:

- Is the test meaningful?
- Is the test easy to read and understand?
- Is the test tightly tied to a particular implementation?

This last point is particularly important.

For a test to be of value, it must enable refactoring; tests that are tied to one particular way of solving the problem often have negative value because they must be modified or rewritten whenever the code is changed. Unfortunately, it is easy to write tests in this way for a number of months or years before you realize you were doing it wrong.

By concentrating on the one property that is easy to measure, the others are de-emphasized. But, much worse than this, trying to meet a coverage target can actively push developers towards writing tests that are tied to the implementation. Bad tests are easier to write than good tests.

It is probably fair to say that there is a problem when code has only 30% unit test coverage. On the other hand, if coverage is achieved by setting a target, code with 80% coverage may be harder to work with than code with a lower figure.

So don't set targets, instead make sure your team is committed to writing good tests.

A good test is one which helps explains the code, catches regression and doesn't get in the way when changes are made. Writing the tests before the code can help encourage good tests and will ensure that code has high coverage.

Style

There are many aspects to programming style, from the mundane questions of where to place braces and new lines through to the more interesting questions of how you design and structure your code.

This section looks at all of these aspects, starting with the more abstract concerns before drilling down to the more concrete.

Although static analysis tools can measure aspects of many of the things discussed in most cases they cannot make break-the-build decisions about whether the code is good. A skilled human is required to make trade offs and apply discretion.

Summary

Code generators can automatically implement certain types of functionality, saving time and eliminating the possibility of certain classes of bugs.

Although they have much to recommend them, code generators also have a cost that should be considered carefully before incorporating them into your project.

Favor generators that allow a clear separation between generated and non-generated functionality, but make sure you understand the trade-offs you are making before including any generator into your project.

Details

Code generators can be grouped into three general types:

- Boilerplate generators
- Compile time annotation processors
- Runtime generators/frameworks

Boilerplate Generators

Boilerplate generators are the simplest form of code generation. They can be further split into :

- Generators that insert code into existing classes (e.g. methods auto generated by an IDE).
- Generators that produce scaffolding that is checked into version control and modified.
- Generators that produce new classes from a model. The generated code is not normally checked into version control.

We recommend that the first type are using sparingly, if at all. This is discussed further in "Know How to Implement Hashcode and Equals".

Generating code from a model (such as a schema or grammar) can be a useful approach as long as the generated code is not modified and is packaged separately. If generated and non-generated code are packaged within the same module then this can start to cause friction (see below).

Compile Time Annotation Processors

JSR 269 introduced a standard framework for processing annotations at build time. Several tools exist that use JSR 269 to generate code.

Most use the annotated classes purely as input, from which new classes are generated. Often, the new classes extend or implement the annotated class or interface but remain separate. These are really just a subset of model based boilerplate generators where the model input model is annotated Java classes.

Some (such as project Lombok) update the annotated classes themselves, adding additional behavior. This is likely to increase both surprise and friction which are discussed below.

Downsides

There are clearly a lot of upsides to code generators, so why wouldn't they always make sense?

The main issues they cause are *surprise* and *friction*.

Surprise

If you generate code at compile or runtime the you are no longer programming in Java.

You are programming in an augmented Java that does things that developers maintaining the code may not be aware of.

It may do things that they do not expect.

It may break fundamental assumptions that programmers have about what can or cannot happen within their code.

Runtime generators will usually generate more surprise than compile time systems - they add an element of *magic* that breaks the usual Java rules. Runtime generators also often weaken type safety, moving classes of problem a developer would normally expect to occur at compile time to runtime.

The first time a developer encounters a code generator in a project, everything it does will be surprising.

After a period of learning, most of the surprise should go away but each developer will need to go through this learning period. The learning involved can be significant - gaining a complete understanding of framework such as Spring is, for example, a significant effort.

The most worrying problem is when there is still some surprise left after the initial learning period.

If you find yourself asking the question "could this be because of the code generator?" when something unexpected happens with your system, and having to eliminate that possibility each time, then you have introduced a very real cost into your project.

Friction

Code using compile-time generators will not import cleanly into IDEs unless the IDE understands how to run the generator. Even when the system is supported by an IDE it may require plugins to be installed, configuration options to be set etc.

The amount of friction, and how often it is encountered, will depend on the IDE and the quality of the support. There may be little friction and it may only be encountered when a new developer joins a project. Or it may be considerable and triggered each time code is cleaned.

The most effective way to reduce the friction is to package the generated code separately from the code that depends upon it. The generated code then becomes a normal binary dependency and the fact that it is automated becomes an internal implementation detail.

While this works well, it may also have a downside. It may create artificial modules. If the code was not auto-generated, would it have made sense to package it as a separate module?

Runtime generators do not usually introduce much friction, although sometimes issues might be experienced if javaagents are not present when running tests from the IDE.

The Trade-off

So those are the issues.

Surprise and friction sound like minor concerns compared to the promise of functionality for free, but their impact can be significant.

Whether or not it makes sense to introduce a code generator often depends on how much it will be used. If there is a large amount of functionality that can be auto-generated then it probably makes sense, if the amount is relatively small it may be best to stick with vanilla Java.

Optimize for Readability not Performance

Summary

Don't optimize your code prematurely.

Concentrate on making it simple and understandable instead.

Details

Many new programmers worry about the performance of each method they write, avoid code they expect to be inefficient and write in a style that attempts to minimize object allocations, method calls, assignments or other factors they expect to have a cost.

Although it often decreases readability and increases complexity, most micro-performance optimization provides no performance benefit at all.

Within the context in which we work, performance should be one of the concerns considered last. Instead, attention should be paid to making code as simple and readable as possible.

If a performance issue arises, profiling should be used to identify where the problems actually lie.

This does not mean the performance should be disregarded completely, but it should always be trumped by code readability and simplicity until it can be proven that there is a real benefit to optimization. Where code can be written in a more efficient manner without **any** increase in complexity or trade-off with readability then the (presumed) more efficient code should be preferred.

Prefer Readable Code to Comments

Summary

Use comments only to explain what you cannot make the code itself explain.

If you are about to write a comment, first think if there is a way you could change the code so that it would be understandable without comments.

Details

From Clean Code by Robert C Martin.

"Nothing can be quite so helpful as a well-placed comment. Nothing can clutter up a module more than frivolous dogmatic comments. Nothing can be quite so damaging as an old crufty comment that propagates lies and misinformation."

Comments should be used only to explain the intent behind code that cannot be refactored to explain itself.

Bad

```
// Check to see if the employee is eligible for full benefits
if ((employee.flags & HOURLY_FLAG) &&
(employee.age > 65))
```

Better

```
if (employee.isEligibleForFullBenefits())
```

A comment is only useful if it explains something that the code itself cannot.

This means that any comments you do write should provide the **why**, not the what or the how

Bad

```
// make sure the port is greater or equal to 1024
if (port < 1024) {
  throw new InvalidPortError(port);
}
```

Better

```
// port numbers below 1024 (the privileged or "well-known ports")
// require root access, which we don't have
if (port < 1024) {
  throw new InvalidPortError(port);
}
```

Better still

```
if (requiresRootPrivileges(port)) {
  throw new InvalidPortError(port);
}

private boolean requiresRootPrivileges(int port) {
  // port numbers below 1024 (the privileged or "well-known ports")
  // require root access on unix systems
  return port < 1024;
}
```

Here, the functional intent has been captured in the method name, the comment has been used solely to provide some context as to why the logic makes sense.

The magic number might also be replaced with a constant.

```
final static const HIGHEST_PRIVILEDGED_PORT = 1023;

private boolean requiresRootPrivileges(int port) {
  // The privileged or "well-known ports" require root access on unix systems
  return port <= HIGHEST_PRIVILEDGED_PORT;
}
```

The comment arguably still adds value however - if nothing else it gives a reader unfamiliar with the topic two key phrases to search for on the web.

Javadoc Judiciously

Summary

Javadoc can help document code but often there are better ways to do so. Think carefully before deciding to write it.

Details

Javadoc is Good

Javadoc is invaluable for external teams that must consume your code without access to the source.

All externally consumed code should have javadoc for its public methods.

Ensure that all such javadoc concentrates on *what* a method does, not *how* it does it.

Javadoc is Bad

Javadoc duplicates information that ought to be clear from the code itself and carries a constant maintenance cost.

If it is not updated in tandem with the code then it becomes misleading.

Do not Javadoc code that will be consumed and maintained only by your immediate team. Instead spend effort ensuring that the code speaks for itself.

Remember KISS and YAGNI

Summary

Keep your design as simple as possible.

Create only the functionality you need now - not what you think you might need in the future.

Details

The KISS (Keep It Simple, Stupid) and YAGNI (You Ain't Going To Need It) acronyms provide good advice that is worth remembering while coding.

KISS advises that we keep our code and designs as simple as possible.

Few people would disagree with this, but unfortunately it is not always obvious what *simple* means.

Given two solutions to a problem which one is simpler?

- The one with the least lines of code?
- The one with the least number of classes?
- The one that uses fewer third party dependencies?
- The one with fewer branch statements?
- The one where the logic is most explicit?
- The one which is consistent with a solution used elsewhere?

All of the above are reasonable definitions of *simple*. None of them is the single definition always makes sense to follow.

Recognizing simple isn't easy and keeping things simple takes a lot of work.

If we could somehow measure the complexity of our software, we would find that there is some minimum value that each piece of software must contain.

If the software were any simpler, then it would be less functional.

Real programs will always contain this *inherent complexity* plus a bit. This extra complexity is the *accidental complexity* we have added because we are less than perfect.

Telling accidental complexity apart from inherent complexity is of course also hard.

Fortunately YAGNI gives us some useful advice on how to keep things simple without having to tell accidental and inherent complexity apart.

The more a system does, the higher its overall complexity will be. If we make a system that does less, it will be simpler - it will have less *inherent complexity* and less *accidental complexity*

Your goal is, therefore, to create the minimum amount of functionality that solves the problems you have right **now**.

- Don't implement things because you think you might need them later. Implement in the future if you need it.
- Don't try and make things "flexible" or "configurable". Make them do just what they need to do - parameterize them at the point you have a need to do so.

If you create more than the minimum amount of functionality, you will have more code to debug, understand and maintain from that point forward until someone has the confidence to delete it.

Prefer Composition to Inheritance

Summary

Composition usually results in more flexible designs.

First consider using composition, then fall back to using inheritance only when composition does not seem to be a good fit.

Details

Composition means building things by adding other things together. Inheritance is building things by extending behavior based on an existing class by creating a child classes.

To take a minimal example- If there is a requirement for a class to accept and store String values, some programmers new to Java will reach for inheritance as follows:

```
class InheritanceAbuse extends ArrayList<String> {

  public void performBusinessLogic(int i) {
    // do things with stored strings
  }

}
```

The same functionality can be implemented using composition.

```
class UsesComposition {

  private final List<String> values = new ArrayList<String>();

  public void performBusinessLogic(int i) {
    // do things with stored strings
  }

  public void add(String value) {
    this.values.add(value);
  }

}
```

Despite requiring more code, an experienced Java programmer would not even consider the first approach. So why is it that the second version is preferable?

There are several overlapping explanations, we'll start with the most abstract and move on to more practical ones.

Inheritance is a Strong Relationship

Inheritance is used to model an IS-A relationship - i.e. we are saying that our `InheritanceAbuse` class is an ArrayList and we should be able to pass one to any piece of code that accepts an ArrayList.

Composition creates a HAS-A relationship; this is a weaker relationship and we should always favor weaker relationships in our code.

So favoring composition over inheritance is just one specific instance of the more general advice to favor weak relationships between our classes.

Using inheritance makes sense when there is an IS-A relationship there but it is an inappropriate mechanism to use purely for reusing code.

Inheritance Breaks Encapsulation

The inheritance implementation fails to encapsulate an implementation detail - that we're storing things in an ArrayList.

The interface to our class includes all sort of methods from ArrayList such as:

- clear
- remove
- contains

Do these methods make sense for our class? If someone calls them, could it interfere with the logic in `performBusinessLogic` ?

We don't know enough about what our example class is meant to do to answer these questions definitively, but the answer is most likely that we would prefer not to expose these methods.

If we switch from ArrayList to some other list implementation this is visible to the classes clients. Code that previously compiled may now break even if no methods specific to ArrayList are called - the change of type alone might cause compilation failures.

We Can Only Do This Once

Java doesn't support multiple inheritance so we only get to pick one thing to extend. If our class also needed to store Integers then inheritance isn't even an option so we'd have to use composition.

Composition is inherently more flexible in single inheritance languages.

Composition Aids Testing

This is not relevant to our simple example, but it is trivial to test how classes linked together by composition interact. It is far harder when inheritance is used.

```
class MyUntestableClass extends SomeDependency {
  public void performBusinessLogic(int i) {
    // do things using methods from SomeDependency
  }
}


class MyClass {
  private final SomeDependency dependency;

  MyClass(SomeDependency dependency) {
    this.dependency = dependency;
  }

  public void performBusinessLogic(int i) {
    // do things with dependency
  }
}
```

It is easy to inject a mock into `MyClass` . Tricks exist to isolate the code in `MyUntestableClass` from `SomeDependency` for the purpose of unit testing, but they are far more involved.

Inheritance is Static

Inheritance sets a fixed relationship between concrete classes at compile time. With composition it is possible to swap in different concrete classes at runtime.

Again composition is inherently more flexible.

Interface Inheritance

The advice to prefer composition to inheritance refers to *implementation inheritance* (i.e. extending a class). The disadvantages discussed above do not apply to *interface inheritance* (i.e. implementing an interface).

In fact, the design choice you often have to make is between implementation inheritance or a combination of composition and interface inheritance.

In these situations, the advice is still to prefer the approach that uses composition.

For example, the well known composition based Decorator pattern:

```
class ProcessorUpperCaseDecorator implements Processor {

  private final Processor child;

  ProcessorUpperCaseDecorator(Processor child) {
    this.child = child;
  }

  @Override
  public void process(String someString) {
    child.process(someString.toUpperCase());
  }

}
```

Could also be implemented using inheritance

```
class InheritanceUpperCaseDecorator extends ConcreteProcessor {

  @Override
  public void process(String someString) {
    super.process(someString.toUpperCase());
  }

}
```

But, again, this solution would be less flexible.

With the composition based version we can decorate any `Processor`. With the inheritance version we would need to re-implement the decorator for each concrete type to which we wished to add the upper case behavior.

Many common OO patterns rely on the combination of Composition and interface inheritance.

When to Use Implementation Inheritance

Almost anything that can be achieved with implementation inheritance can also be achieved using the combination of interface inheritance and composition.

So when should implementation inheritance be used?

Implementation inheritance has one single advantage over composition - it's less verbose.

So implementation inheritance should be used when **both** of the following conditions are met

1. There is an IS-A relationship to be modelled
2. The composition based approach would result in too much boilerplate code

The 2nd point is unfortunately entirely subjective.

Keep It SOLID

Summary

The SOLID acronym provides some guidance on design that you should follow.

- **S**ingle Responsibility Principle
- **O**pen Closed Principle
- **L**iskov Substitution Principle
- **I**nterface Segregation Principle
- **D**ependency Inversion Principle

Details

Single Responsibility Principle

Separate your concerns - a class should do one thing and one thing only. To put it another way, a class should have a single reason to change.

Open / Closed Principle

You should be able to extend behavior, without modifying existing code.

".. you should design modules that never change. When requirements change, you extend the behavior of such modules by adding new code, not by changing old code that already works."

— *Robert Martin*

An indication that you might not be following this principle is the presence of `switch` statements or `if/else` logic in your code.

Liskov Substitution Principle

Derived classes must be substitutable for their base classes.

One indication that you are breaking this principle is the presence of `instanceof` statements in your code.

Interface Segregation Principle

The Interface Segregation Principle states that clients should not be forced to implement interfaces they don't use; prefer small, tailored interfaces to large, catch-all ones.

One indication that you might be breaking this principle is the presence of empty methods or methods throwing `OperationNotSupportedException` in your code.

Dependency Inversion Principle

High-level modules should not depend upon low-level modules. Both should depend upon abstractions.

Abstractions should never depend upon details. Details should depend upon abstractions.

In practice this means you should follow one of two patterns:

1. Package the interfaces a 'high-level' component depends upon with that component
2. Package the interface a component depends upon separately from both the client and implementation

This first approach is classic dependency inversions (contrast it with the traditional approach of have the high level component depend upon the lower layers).

The second approach is known as the "Separated Interface Pattern". It is a little more heavy weight, but also more flexible as it makes no assumption about who should own the interface.

An indication that you are breaking this principle is the presence of package cycles within your code.

Keep Your Code DRY

Summary

Don't Repeat Yourself (DRY) - avoid writing the same logic more than once.

Every time you copy and paste code, flick yourself in the eye. This is a great disincentive to doing it again but over time may cause blindness.

Details

If the same logic is required more than once then it should not be duplicated; it should instead, be extracted to a well named class or method.

This will be both easier to read and easier to maintain because a change will only be required in one place should the logic need to change.

Bad

```
class Foo {
   private int status;
   private boolean approved;

   foo() {
     if (status == 12 || approved) {
       doFoo();
     }
   }

   bar() {
     if (status == 12 || approved) {
       doBar();
     }
   }
}
```

Better

```
class Foo {
  private final static int PRE_APPROVED = 12;

  private int status;
  private boolean approved;

  foo() {
    if (isApproved()) {
      doFoo();
    }
  }

  bar() {
    if (isApproved()) {
      doBar();
    }
  }

  private isApproved() {
    return status == PRE_APPROVED || approved;
  }
}
```

Things are a little trickier when we have similar but not identical logic.

Although it is quick and easy, the worst thing we can do is copy and paste.

Terrible

```
public void doSomething(List<Widget> widgets) {
  for (Widget widget : widgets) {
    reportExistence(widget);
    if (widget.snortles() > 0) {
      reportDeviance(widget);
      performSideEffect(widget);
    }
  }
}

public void doSomethingSimilar(List<Widget> widgets) {
  for (Widget widget : widgets) {
    reportExistence(widget);
    if (widget.snortles() > 0) {
      reportDeviance(widget);
      performDifferentSideEffect(widget);
    }
  }
}
```

This seemed quick and easy now, but is the start of a codebase that will suck time each time we try to understand or change it.

A straightforward but very limited approach to re-use code is to introduce Boolean flags.

Not great

```
public void doSomething(List<Widget> widgets) {
  doThings(widgets, false);
}

public void doSomethingSimilar(List<Widget> widgets) {
  doThings(widgets, true);
}


private void doThings(List<Widget> widgets, boolean doDifferentSideEffect) {
  for (Widget widget : widgets) {
    reportExistence(widget);
    if (widget.snortles() > 0) {
      reportDeviance(widget);
      if (doDifferentSideEffect) {
        performDifferentSideEffect(widget);
      } else {
        performSideEffect(widget);
      }
    }
  }
}
```

This is ugly and gets worse as the number of possibilities increases.

A much more scalable approach is to use the Strategy pattern.

If we introduce an interface:

```
interface WidgetAction {
   void apply(Widget widget);
}
```

Then we can use it as follows:

Better

```
public void doSomething(List<Widget> widgets) {
  doThings(widgets, performSideEffect());
}


public void doSomethingSimilar(List<Widget> widgets) {
  doThings(widgets, performDifferentSideEffect());
}

private WidgetAction performSideEffect() {
  return new WidgetAction() {
    @Override
    public void apply(Widget widget) {
      performSideEffect(widget);
    }
  };
}

private WidgetAction performDifferentSideEffect() {
  return new WidgetAction() {
    @Override
    public void apply(Widget widget) {
      performDifferentSideEffect(widget);
    }
  };
}

private void doThings(List<Widget> widgets, WidgetAction action ) {
  for (Widget widget : widgets) {
    reportExistence(widget);
    if (widget.snortles() > 0) {
      reportDeviance(widget);
      action.apply(widget);
    }
  }
}
```

The Java 7 version is quite verbose due to the anonymous inner class boiler plate.

Arguably, Boolean flags might be preferable for very simple cases such as this but, if we extract the logic in `performSideEffect` and `performDifferentSideEffect` methods into top-level classes implementing `WidgetAction` , then the Strategy version becomes compelling.

In Java 8, there is little question that the Strategy pattern is preferable in even the simplest of cases.

Better with Java 8

```
public void doSomething(List<Widget> widgets) {
  doThings(widgets, widget -> performSideEffect(widget));
}

public void doSomethingSimilar(List<Widget> widgets) {
  doThings(widgets, widget -> performDifferentSideEffect(widget));
}

private void doThings(List<Widget> widgets, Consumer<Widget> action ) {
  for (Widget widget : widgets) {
    reportExistence(widget);
    if (widget.snortles() > 0) {
      reportDeviance(widget);
      action.accept(widget);
    }
  }
}
```

We do not need to introduce our own interface - the built-in `Consumer<T>` is enough. We should consider introducing one if the `doThings` method were exposed publicly or if the logic in `performSideEffect` was complex enough to pull into a top-level class.

The loop might also be converted to a pipeline.

As a pipeline

```
private void doThings(List<Widget> widgets, Consumer<Widget> action ) {
  widgets
  .stream()
  .peek(widget -> reportExistence(widget))
  .filter(widget -> widget.snortles() > 0)
  .peek(widget -> reportDeviance(widget))
  .forEach(action);
}
```

Prefer Reversible Decisions

Summary

Prefer design decisions that will be easy to change.

Details

Many of the decisions you make while designing your code will eventually turn out to be wrong.

If you can make your decisions reversible by containing their consequences and adding abstractions then this future change will not matter.

For example - if you introduce a third party library and reference it throughout your code, then you have made high the cost of reversing the decision to use that library. If you constrain it to a single location and create an interface for it, the cost of reversing the decision is low.

But don't forget KISS and YAGNI - if your abstractions complicate the design then it is better to leave them out.

Make Dependencies Explicit and Visible

Summary

Make sure that the dependencies of a class are clearly visible.

Always inject dependencies into a class using its constructor. Do not use other methods such as setters or annotations on fields.

Never introduce dependencies using hidden routes such as `Singletons` or `ThreadLocals`.

Details

Code is easier to understand if the interfaces and classes that each object depends on are conspicuous and visible.

The most visible dependencies are the ones that are injected into a method as a parameter.

Less visible are the ones stored as fields but, depending on how those fields are populated, the dependencies can still be relatively easy to discover.

Constructor Injection

Constructor dependency injection clearly communicates an object's dependencies in a single location and ensures objects are only ever created in valid states. It allows fields to be made **final** so that their life cycle is unambiguous.

This is the only way in which dependencies should be injected.

Setter Injection

Setter injection increases the number of possible states an object could be in. Many of those states will be invalid.

If setter injection is used, a class can be constructed in a half-initialized state. What constitutes a fully-initialized state can only be determined by examining the code.

Bad

```
public class Foo() {
  private Bar bar;

  public void doStuff() {
    bar.doBarThings();
  }

  public void setBar(Bar bar) {
    this.bar = bar;
  }
}
```

Here, a `NullPointerException` will be thrown if `Foo` is constructed without calling `setBar`.

Better

```
public class Foo() {
  private final Bar bar;

  public Foo(Bar bar) {
    this.bar = bar;
  }

  public void doStuff() {
    bar.doBarThings();
  }
}
```

Here, it is clear that we must supply a `Bar` as we are unable to construct the class without it.

Field Annotations

While annotations on fields seem convenient they mean that the dependency will not be visible in the public API. They also tie construction of your class to the frameworks that understand them and prevent fields from being made final.

Field annotations should not be used.

If you are working with a dependency injection framework such as Spring, either move construction of your objects into configuration classes or restrict the use on annotations to constructors. Both methods allow your classes to be constructed normally and ensure that all dependencies are visible.

Hidden Dependencies

Anything that is not injected into a class using a constructor or as a method parameter is a hidden dependency.

These are evil.

They are pulled in from `Singletons` , `ThreadLocals` , static method calls or by simply calling `new` .

Bad

```
public class HiddenDependencies {
  public void doThings() {
    Connection connection = Database.getInstance().getConnection();
    // do things with connection
    ....
  }
}
```

Here we must ensure that the `Database` class is in a valid state before calling the `doThings` method of the code below, but we have no way of knowing this without looking through every line of code.

Better

```
public class HiddenDependencies {
  private final Database database;

  public HiddenDependencies(Database database) {
    this.database = database;
  }

  public void doThings() {
    Connection connection = database.getConnection();
    // do things with connection
    ....
  }
}
```

Injecting via the constructor makes the dependency clearly visible.

By definition, hidden dependencies are hard to discover but they have a second issue - they are also hard to replace.

Seams

Seams are a concept introduced by Michael Feathers in "Working Effectively with legacy code"

He defines it as:

> "a place where you can alter behavior in your program without editing in that place."

In the original version of `HiddenDependencies` if we wanted to replace `Database` with a mock or stub we could only do so if the singleton provided some method to modify the instance it returns.

Not a good approach

```
public class Database implements IDatabase {
  private static IDatabase instance = new Database();

  public static IDatabase getInstance() {
    return instance;
  }

  public static void setInstanceForTesting(IDatabase database) {
    instance = database;
  }

}
```

This approach introduces a seam but does not address our concerns around visibility. The dependency remains hidden.

If we used this approach, our codebase would remain hard to understand and we would find ourselves constantly fighting test order dependencies.

With constructor injection, we gain a seam and make the dependency visible. Even if `Database` is a singleton, we are still able to isolate our code from it for testing.

Prefer Immutable Objects

Summary

Where possible, create objects that cannot be changed - especially if those objects will be long-lived or globally accessible.

Details

Mutable state makes programs harder to understand and maintain.

When objects are short-lived, and do not leave method scope, mutable state causes few problems. Writes and reads will be close together and there will be a clear order in which this happens.

For longer-lived objects, things are more complex.

If an object escapes from a method then it may be accessed from more than one location within the code.

We must start by assuming that anything that can happen to these objects will. We can only confirm that certain situations do not occur by examining the whole program.

The set of things that might happen to an immutable object is far smaller than for a mutable one. By constraining how long lived objects can behave we have made things simpler. There are fewer possibilities that we must consider.

Unfortunately, it is not always easy to tell from a class definition what the lifecycle of objects of that type will be. Perhaps only short-lived instances will be created. Perhaps only long-lived ones. Perhaps a mixture of the two.

If we design immutable classes by default we do not need to worry about this.

The Problem With Mutable Objects

If we have a very simple class such as `Foo`

```
public class Foo {
  private Long id;

  public Long getId() {
    return id;
  }

  public void setId(Long id) {
    this.id = id;
  }

  @Override
  public int hashCode() {
    return Objects.hashCode(id);
  }

  @Override
  public boolean equals(Object obj) {
    if (this == obj)
      return true;
    if (obj == null)
      return false;
    if (getClass() != obj.getClass())
      return false;
    Foo other = (Foo) obj;
    return Objects.equals(id, other.id);
  }
}
```

We would need to search our codebase for all usages of it to establish the following :

It is Never Accessed from Multiple Threads

`Foo` is not thread safe.

Writes to longs are not atomic and nothing within `Foo` itself establishes a happens-before relationship between the field write and read.

If `setId` and `getId` are ever called from different threads we might get back stale or garbage values.

`setId` Is Never Called After `Foo` Has Been Placed in a Set

The `hashcode` of this class relies on a mutable field. If we modify it after we place it in a set then our program will not behave as we expect.

The Flow of Our Data

Even if our program behaves correctly, we need to do work in order to understand how it functions.

`setId` can be called at any point after the object is created. We can, therefore, only understand how data flows through our program by looking for all calls to `setId` - perhaps there are several, perhaps there is only one. The only way we can discover this is by examining the entire program.

Immutable Objects

If we can make our objects immutable we gain guarantees that mean we do not need to worry about how our objects are used.

```
@Immutable
public final class Foo {
  private final Long id;

  public Foo(Long id) {
    this.id = id;
  }

  public Long getId() {
    return id;
  }

  @Override
  public int hashCode() {
    return Objects.hashCode(id);
  }

  @Override
  public boolean equals(Object obj) {
    if (this == obj)
      return true;
    if (obj == null)
      return false;
    if (getClass() != obj.getClass())
      return false;
    Foo other = (Foo) obj;
    return Objects.equals(id, other.id);
  }
}
```

It no longer matters if `Foo` is long or short lived.

It is inherently thread-safe.

We know that whatever value we construct it with will remain until it dies. There is only one possible point where data is written so we do not need to search for others.

Annotations

The example uses the JSR3051 `javax.annotation.concurrent.Immutable` annotation.

This does not in any way change the object's functionality but provides a way to communicate the intent of this being an immutable class. Static analysis tools such as Mutablility Detector can check if this intent has been violated.

We can tell at a glance that `Foo` is immutable as it has final fields of a well known immutable type.

The `final` keyword ensures only that the reference a field points to will not change.

If the field were of type `Bar` then we would not know if it were mutable or not without examining `Bar` to see if it too were immutable. Even if we were not using a static analysis tool the use of the `Immutable` annotation would make this assessment faster.

Instead of updating the state of immutable objects, we create new instances that retain the state we do not wish to modify.

This pattern seems strange to some Java programmers at first, but the programming model is similar to how the familiar `String` class works.

```
@Immutable
public final class Bar {
  private int anInt;
  private String aString;

  public Bar(int anInt, String aString) {
    this.anInt = anInt;
    this.aString = aString;
  }


  @CheckReturnValue
  public Bar withAnInt(int anInt) {
    return new Bar(anInt, this.aString);
  }

  @CheckReturnValue
  public Bar withAString(String aString) {
    return new Bar(this.antInt, aString);
  }
}
```

Instances of `Bar` with new values can be obtained by calling `withAString` and `withAnInt` .

The JSR305 `javax.annotation.CheckReturnValue` enables static analysis tools such as Error Prone to issue a warning if a mistake is made such as in the code below.

```
public Bar doThings(Bar bar) {
  if(someLogic()) {
    bar.withAnInt(42);
  }
  return bar;
}
```

The call here to `withAnInt` achieves nothing because the return value is not stored. Most likely, the programmer intended to write:

```
public Bar doThings(Bar bar) {
  if(someLogic()) {
    return bar.withAnInt(42);
  }
  return bar;
}
```

When to Use Mutable Objects

Mutable objects require slightly less boilerplate to create than immutable ones.

If you know that a class will only ever be used to create short-lived, local objects then you might consider making it mutable. But you must weigh this against the additional work required to ensure that the class is only ever used in this fashion as the codebase grows.

Options exist to auto-generate both immutable and mutable classes, thereby removing mutable objects' main advantage. Two of these options are discussed further in "Know How to Implement Hashcode and Equals".

Mutable objects used to be the norm in Java. As a result, many common frameworks require mutable objects. Persistence and serialization frameworks often require Java beans with no args constructors and setters. Other frameworks might require you to use two-stage construction with a lifecycle method such as init.

It is not always highlighted in the documentation but some long standing frameworks have been updated to support immutable objects.

Jackson for example now allows constructors and factory methods to be annotated :-

```
public class Foo  {
  private final int x
  private final int y;

  @JsonCreator
  public Foo(@JsonProperty("x") int x, @JsonProperty("y") int y) {
   this.x = x;
   this.y = y;
  }
}
```

Other frameworks, such as Hibernate, can only be used with classes that provide a default constructor. Although they can be configured to set fields directly without the need for setters this causes more problems than it solves.

If you are tied to a framework that requires mutability then you will need to use mutable objects where you interface with that framework.

Use a Consistent Code Layout Within Each Project

Summary

Agree and enforce a standard code formatting scheme within each codebase.

Detail

The way in which Java code is formatted and laid out is largely a matter of personal preference.

Some styles (such as omitting braces in conditional statements) can arguably make certain types of bug slightly more likely.

Others might require more work to keep the code compliant (such as aligning fields into columns) but, to a first approximation, no particular scheme is greatly superior to any other.

Despite this, programmers tend to have strong opinions on the matter.

Every codebase should, however, have a single agreed formatting style which is consistently applied and is understood by everyone working on that codebase.

This prevents commit wars in which different team members re-format things to their personal preference. It also makes code easier to understand as there is a cognitive cost for the reader if formatting changes radically from file to file.

Although there is value in consistency, there is also a cost.

Unless there is already broad agreement across teams about how things should be formatted, trying to enforce one official set of rules is likely to create more ill will than benefit.

A global preferred reference should therefore be set, but teams should be free to deviate from this as they see fit as long as a consistent style is used for the code they maintain.

Suggested Formatting Rules

If your do not have your own strong preferences we suggest you follow the Google Java Style.

These formatting rules are well thought out, clearly documented and not overly prescriptive.

We will not describe them in any detail here, but code formatted to these rules will look something like the following :-

```
class Example {
  int[] myArray = {1, 2, 3, 4, 5, 6};
  int theInt = 1;
  String someString = "Hello";
  double aDouble = 3.0;

  void foo(int a, int b, int c, int d, int e, int f) {
    if (f == 5) {
      System.out.println("fnord");
    } else {
      System.out.println(someString);
    }

    switch (a) {
      case 0:
        Other.doFoo();
        break;
      default:
        Other.doBaz();
    }
  }

  void bar(List<Integer> v) {
    for (int i = 0; i < 10; i++) {
      v.add(new Integer(i));
    }
  }
}
```

However, we suggest that the guidance in the Google guide on when to write Javadoc is ignored in favor of our own.

Notable Points About This Style

Spaces not Tabs

Tabs may appear differently depending on how an editor is configured. This will result in constant reformatting as different programmers adapt the file to their editor settings. Spaces avoid this problem.

In some languages (e.g. JavaScript before the rise of code minifiers) tabs have/had an advantage as they reduced the size of the source file compared to using multiple spaces. The increase in size of the source file is of no relevance for Java.

One True Brace Style

There are various arguments about the supposed advantages of this style, but we suggest its use mainly because it is common in the Java community.

Although simple `if else` statements can be more concisely written by omitting the braces we suggest that they are always included. This reduces the chance of a statement being placed outside the conditional when this was not the intent.

Group Methods for Easy Comprehension

Summary

The public methods of a class should appear at the top of the file, the private methods towards the bottom and any protected or package default methods in between.

In addition to arranging by accessibility, they should also be ordered into a logical flow.

Detail

This scheme tries to achieve two goals:

1. Highlight the public API by separating it from implementation detail
2. Allow the reader to follow the logical flow with the minimal of scrolling

To achieve the 2nd goal, methods should be arranged into logical groups, with methods always appearing above the ones they call.

The two goals clearly conflict because grouping the public API methods together at the top of the file prevents grouping them with the implementation methods that they used. If this causes a large problem it may be an indication that the class has too many responsibilities and could be refactored into one or more smaller classes.

Questions of the "correct" location of a method will also occur when an implementation method is called from multiple locations or methods have recursive relationships. There is, of course, no one right answer and any ordering that broadly meets the second goal may be used.

Constructors and static factory methods should usually be placed first in the class. The fact that a method is static should not, however, generally influence where it is placed.

Example

```
public class Layout {

  private int a;

  Layout() {...}

  public static Layout create() {...}

  public void api1() {
    if (...) {
      doFoo();
    }
  }

  public void api2() {
    if(...) {
      doBar();
    }
  }

  private void doFoo() {
    while(...) {
      handleA();
      handleB();
    }
    leaf();
  }

  private void handleA() {...}

  private void handleB() {...}

  private static void doBar() {
    if (...) {
      leaf();
    }
  }

  private void leaf() {...}
}
```

Fields should always be placed at the top of the class before any methods.

Keep Methods Small and Simple

Summary

Keep methods small and simple.

Details

Small things are easier to understand than big things. Methods are no different.

One way to measure the size of a method is via the number of lines of code it contains.

As a guide methods should not usually be longer than 7 lines in length. This is not a hard rule - just a guide of when to feel uncomfortable with a method's size.

Another way to gauge the size of a method is to see how many possible paths there are through it. The *Cyclomatic complexity* of a method gives a measure of this - it will increase as the amount of conditional logic and number of loops grows.

As a guide, methods should not usually have a complexity above 5. Again, this is not a hard rule, just a guide of when to feel uncomfortable.

Your code will naturally contain some methods that are larger than others - some concepts are inherently more complex than others and the implementation will not become simpler if broken down further or expressed in a different way.

But most large methods can be made smaller in one of three ways :

- Refactoring into a number of smaller methods
- Re-expressing the logic
- Using appropriate language features

Splitting a Method into Smaller Concerns

Many large methods have smaller methods within them trying to find a way out.

We can make our code easier to maintain by freeing them.

Bad

```
protected static Map<String, String> getHttpHeaders(HttpServletRequest request) {
  Map<String, String> httpHeaders = new HashMap<String, String>();

  if (request == null || request.getHeaderNames() == null) {
    return httpHeaders;
  }

  Enumeration names = request.getHeaderNames();

  while (names.hasMoreElements()) {
    String name = (String)names.nextElement();
    String value = request.getHeader(name);
    httpHeaders.put(name.toLowerCase(), value);
  }

  return httpHeaders;
}
```

Better

```
protected static Map<String, String> getHttpHeaders(HttpServletRequest request) {
  if ( isInValidHeader(request) ) {
    return Collections.emptyMap();
  }
  return extractHeaders(request);
}

private static boolean isInValidHeader(HttpServletRequest request) {
  return (request == null || request.getHeaderNames() == null);
}

private static Map<String, String> extractHeaders(HttpServletRequest request) {
  Map<String, String> httpHeaders = new HashMap<String, String>();
  for ( String name : Collections.list(request.getHeaderNames()) ) {
    httpHeaders.put(name.toLowerCase(), request.getHeader(name));
  }
  return httpHeaders;
}
```

Re-expressing logic

Terrible

```
public boolean isFnardy(String item) {
  if (item.equals("AAA")) {
    return true;
  } else if (item.equals("ABA")) {
    return true;
  } else if (item.equals("CC")) {
    return true;
  } else if (item.equals("FWR")) {
    return true;
  } else {
    return false;
  }
}
```

This can be easily re-expressed with less noise as :

Better

```
public boolean isFnardy(String item) {
  return item.equals("AAA")
      || item.equals("ABA")
      || item.equals("CC")
      || item.equals("FWR");
}
```

Or with a move to a more declarative style :

```
private final static Set<String> FNARDY_STRINGS
  = ImmutableSet.of("AAA",
                    "ABA",
                    "CC",
                    "FWR");

public boolean isFnardy(String item) {
  return FNARDY_STRINGS.contains(item);
}
```

Neither of the above changes alter the structure of our program or even affect the signature of the method. Both still reduce both line count and complexity while increasing readability.

Simplifying things with a series of higher impact changes that extract a model of our domain is, however, often the best approach.

It is difficult to guess what this model might look like for our contrived example, but is likely that this conditional logic could be replaced with polymorphism.

```
enum ADomainConcept {
  AAA(true),
  ABA(true),
  CC(true),
  FWR(true),
  OTHER(false),
  ANDANOTHER(false);

  private final boolean isFnardy;
  private ADomainConcept(boolean isFnardy) {
    this.isFnardy = isFnardy;
  }

  boolean  isFnardy() {
    return isFnardy;
  }
}
```

Using Appropriate Language Features

Methods are sometimes bloated by boilerplate that solves common programming problems. The need for some of this boilerplate has been removed by new language features.

Some of these *new* features aren't all that new, but code is still written without them:

- Java 5 Generics removes the need for ugly casts
- The Java 5 for-each-loop can replace code using iterators and indexed loops
- The Java 7 try-with-resources can replace complex try, catch finally blocks
- The Java 7 multi-catch can replace repeated catch blocks
- Java 8 lambda expressions can replace anonymous class boilerplate

Methods Should Do Only One Thing

Summary

Methods should do only one thing.

Details

A useful guide as to whether a function is doing only one thing is given in "Clean Code" by Robert C Martin.

"another way to know that a function is doing more than “one thing” is if you can extract another function from it with a name that is not merely a restatement of its implementation."

Bad

```
public void updateFooStatusAndRepository(Foo foo) {
   if ( foo.hasFjord() ) {
      this.repository(foo.getIdentifier(), this.collaborator.calculate(foo));
   }

   if (importantBusinessLogic()) {
     foo.setStatus(FNAGLED);
     this.collaborator.collectFnagledState(foo);
   }
}
```

Better

```
public void registerFoo(Foo foo) {
   handleFjords(foo);
   updateFnagledState(foo);
}

private void handleFjords(Foo foo) {
    if ( foo.hasFjord() ) {
      this.repository(foo.getIdentifier(), this.collaborator.calculate(foo));
   }
}

private void updateFnagledState(Foo foo) {
  if (importantBusinessLogic()) {
     foo.setStatus(FNAGLED);
     this.collaborator.collectFnagledState(foo);
   }
}
```

You've gone too far

```
public void registerFoo(Foo foo) {
   handleFjords(foo);
   updateFnagledState(foo);
}

private void handleFjords(Foo foo) {
    if ( foo.hasFjord() ) {
      this.repository(foo.getIdentifier(), this.collaborator.calculate(foo));
   }
}

private void updateFnagledState(Foo foo) {
  if (importantBusinessLogic()) {
     updateFooStatus(foo);
     this.collaborator.collectFnagledState(foo);
   }
}

private void updateFooStatus(Foo foo) {
  foo.setStatus(FNAGLED);
}
```

Avoid Null Whenever Possible

Summary

Null is a billion dollar mistake, make sure you know how to avoid using it in your code.

Try to limit the times you or your clients need to write the following:

```
if ( != null ) {
  ...
}
```


Details

Although it is likely that libraries and frameworks you interact with will return null, you should try to ensure that this practice is isolated to third party code.

The core of your application should assume that it does not have to worry about null values.

Strategies to avoid null include :

- The null object pattern - when you have something you think is optional
- The type-safe null pattern (aka Option, Optional & Maybe) - when you need to express that an interface might not return something
- Design by contract

The Null Object Pattern

The null object pattern is the classic OO approach to avoiding null. You should use it whenever you think you have a dependency that you think is optional.

The pattern is very simple, just provide an implementation of the interface that does "nothing" or has a neutral behavior. This can then be safely referenced by its clients, with no need to check for null.

Type-Safe Nulls (aka Optional)

The type-safe null pattern is familiar in most functional programming languages where it is variously known as Maybe, Option or Optional. Java 8 finally adds an Optional type, but implementations are available for earlier versions via Guava and other libraries.

It is a simple pattern. An Optional is basically just a box that can hold either one or zero values. You can check if the box is empty (using `isPresent`) and retrieve its value via a get method.

Optional should be used whenever a public method might not return a value as part of normal program flow.

If you call get on an empty Optional, it will throw a `NoSuchElementException` .

It might not be immediately obvious what value Optional provides over just using null. If you need to check that an Optional has something in it before calling `get` , how is this different from checking a value is not null to avoid a `NullPointerException` ?

There are several important differences.

Firstly, if your method declares that it returns `Optional<Person>` then you can instantly see from the type signature that it might not return a value. If it only returned `Person` you would only know that it might return null if you looked at the source, tests or documentation.

Equally important, if you know that you always return `Optional` within your codebase when something might not be present, then you know at a glance that a method returning `Person` will always return a value and will never return null.

Finally, the preferred way to use Optionals is not to call the get method or to explicitly check if it contains a value. Instead the values that are contained (or not contained) in an Optional can be safely mapped, consumed and filtered by various method on the class.

In the simplest case a possibly empty Optional can be accessed by calling the `orElse` method which takes a default value to use if the Optional is empty.

As mentioned, the sweet spot for using Optionals is for the return types for methods. They should not generally be held as fields (use the null object pattern here instead) or passed to public methods (instead provide overloaded versions that do not require the parameter).

One objection that is sometimes raised by Java programmers encountering Optional for the first time is that it is possible for an Optional to be null itself. While this is true, returning a null Optional from a method is a perverse thing to do and should be considered a coding error.

Static analysis rules exists that can check for code that returns null Optionals.

Design by Contract

We wish for all code that we control to be able to ignore the existence of null (unless it interfaces with some third party code that forces us to consider it).

`Objects.requireNonNull` can be used to add a runtime assertion that null has not been passed to a method.

Because your core code should generally assume that null will never be passed around, there is little value in documenting this behavior with tests; assertions add value because they ensure that an error occurs close to the point where the mistake was made.

We can also check this contract at build time.

JSR-305 provides annotations that can be used to declare where null is acceptable.

Although JSR-305 is dormant, and shows no signs of being incorporated into Java in the near future, the annotations are available at the maven co-ordinates :-

```
<dependency>
    <groupId>com.google.code.findbugs</groupId>
    <artifactId>jsr305</artifactId>
    <version>3.0.1</version>
</dependency>
```

They are supported by several static analysis tools including :-

- Findbugs
- Error Prone

These can be configured to break the build when null is passed as a parameter where we do not expect it.

Annotating every class, method or parameter with `@Nonnull` would quickly become tedious and it would be debatable whether the gain would be worth the amount of noise this would generate.

Fortunately, it is possible to make `@Nonnull` the default by annotating a package in its package-info.java file as follows

```
@javax.annotation.ParametersAreNonnullByDefault
package com.example.somepackage ;
```

Sadly, sub-packages do not inherit their parent's annotations, so a package-info.java file must be created for each package.

Once non null parameters have been made the default behavior, any parameters that do accept null can be annotated with `@Nullable` .

Use Final Liberally

Summary

Consider making final any variable or parameter that does not change.

Details

Making parameters and variables that are assigned once final makes a method easier to understand because it constrains the things that could possibly happen within the code.

It would be reasonable to make all parameters and assign-once variables final, but this needs to be weighed against the noise created by inserting the `final` keyword everywhere.

For short methods, whether the benefit outweighs the cost is arguable, but if a method is large and unwieldy then the case for making things final is much stronger.

Each team should agree a policy for making final variables.

At a minimum, everything should be made final within large methods. This may also be extended to shorter methods at the team's discretion. A blanket policy has the advantage of being easy to automate/understand. A more nuanced policy is harder to communicate.

When working with legacy code, making parameters and variables final is also a useful first step in gaining understanding of the method before re-factoring. Methods that have proved difficult to express in smaller chunks will also become easier to understand when single assignment variables are final.

Provide no More Than One Worker Constructor

Summary

Although a class may provide many constructors, only one should write to fields and initialize the class.

Details

Having a single place where fields are assigned during construction makes it easy to understand the states that class can be constructed in.

Classes should not provide multiple constructors that set fields.

Bad

```
public class Foo {
  private final String a;
  private final Integer b;
  private final Float c;

  public Foo(String value) {
    this.a = Objects.requireNonNull(value);
    this.b = 42;
    this.c = 1.0f;
  }

  public Foo(Integer value) {
    this.a = "";
    this.b = Objects.requireNonNull(value);
    this.c = 1.0f;
  }

  public Foo(Float value) {
    this.a = "";
    this.b = 42;
    this.c = Objects.requireNonNull(value);
  }
}
```

The duplication of values in the above code could be removed but it would remain confusing because the concern of initializing the class is spread across three locations.

If more fields were added it would be easy to forget to initialize them in the existing constructors.

Fortunately, we have made all fields final so this would give a compilation error. If the class was mutable, we would have a bug to discover at runtime.

Better

```
public class Foo {
  private final String a;
  private final Integer b;
  private final Float c;

  private Foo(String a, Integer b, Float c) {
    this.a = Objects.requireNonNull(a);
    this.b = Objects.requireNonNull(b);
    this.c = Objects.requireNonNull(c);
  }

  public Foo(String value) {
    this(value, 42, 1.0f);
  }

  public Foo(Integer value) {
    this("", value, 1.0f);
  }

  public Foo(Float value) {
    this("", 42, value);
  }
}
```

Fields are now only written in one location, resulting in less duplication.

We can also see at a glance that `Foo` cannot be constructed with null values. In the previous version, this could only be determined by scanning three different locations.

Following this pattern, it is difficult to forget to set a field even if it is non-final.

Avoid Checked Exceptions

Summary

Do not declare checked exceptions unless there is a clear course of action that should be taken when one is thrown.

Details

Exceptions are for exceptional circumstances - design your code such that they are not thrown in scenarios that are expected to happen.

This means that they should not be used for normal control flow.

Checked exceptions bloat and complicate code. You should avoid adding them to your API, except when there is a clear action that the caller can always take to recover from the error scenario.

This is surprisingly rare.

If you are working with a library that uses checked exceptions, you can wrap them by re-throwing a runtime exception.

When you do, be sure to maintain the stack trace.

```
try {
  myObject.methodThrowingException();
} catch (SomeCheckedException e) {
  throw new RuntimeException(e);
}
```

If you have caught an `Exception` or a `Throwable` , so are unsure of the exact type, you can avoid creating unnecessary wrappers using Guava's `Throwables.propagate` .

```
try {
  myObject.methodThrowingException();
} catch (Exception e) {
  throw Throwables.propagate(e);
}
```

This will wrap checked exceptions and re-throw unchecked exception as is.

Specifics

This section provides some more specific advice on various Java language features and gotchas.

A lot of what is covered in this section can be automated by tools such as FindBugs, PMD, Checkstyle and Sonar.

Know How to Implement Hashcode and Equals

Summary

Implementing `hashCode` and `equals` is not straightforward. Do not implement them unless it is necessary to do so. If you do implement them, make sure you know what you are doing.

Details

It is well known that if you override equals then you must also override the `hashCode` method (see Effective Java item 9).

If logically-equal objects do not have the same `hashCode` they will behave in a surprising manner if placed in a hash based collection such as `HashMap` .

By "surprising", we mean your program will behave incorrectly in a fashion that is very difficult to debug.

Unfortunately, implementing `equals` is surprisingly hard to do correctly. Effective Java item 8 spends about 12 pages discussing the topic.

The contract for equals is handily stated in the Javadoc of `java.lang.Object` . We will not repeat it here or repeat the discussion of what it means, that can be found in Effective Java and large swathes of the internet. Instead we will look at strategies for implementing it.

Whichever strategy you adopt, it is important that you first write tests for your implementation.

It is easy for an equals method to cause hard-to-diagnose bugs if the code changes (e.g. if fields are added or their type changes). Writing tests for equals methods used to be a painful and time-consuming procedure, but libraries now exist that make it trivial to specify the common cases (see Testing FAQs).

Don't

This is the simplest strategy and the one you should adopt by default in the interests of keeping your codebase small.

Most classes do not need an equals method. Unless your class represents some sort of value it makes little sense to compare it with another so stick with the inherited implementation from Object.

An irritating gray area are classes where the production code never has a requirement to compare equality but the test code does. The dilemma here is whether to implement the methods purely for the benefit of the tests or to complicate the test code with custom equality checks.

There is, of course, no right answer here; we would suggest first trying the compare-it-in-the test approach before falling back to providing a custom equals method.

The custom equality checks can be cleanly shared by implementing a custom assertion using a library such as AssertJ or Hamcrest.

Effective Java tentatively suggests having your class throw an error if equals is unexpectedly called

```
@Override public boolean equals(Object o) {
  throw new AssertionError(); // Method is never called
}
```

This seems like a good idea but, unfortunately, it will confuse most static analysis tools. On balance, it probably creates more problems than it solves.

Auto-Generate With an IDE

Most IDEs provide some method of auto-generating `hashCode` and `equals` methods. This is an easily-accessible approach, but the resulting methods are (depending on the IDE and its settings) often ugly and complex such as the ones generated by Eclipse shown below:

```
@Override
public int hashCode() {
  final int prime = 31;
  int result = 1;
  result = prime * result + ((field1 == null) ? 0 : field1.hashCode());
  result = prime * result + ((field2 == null) ? 0 : field2.hashCode());
  return result;
}
```

```
@Override
public boolean equals(Object obj) {
  if (this == obj)
    return true;
  if (obj == null)
    return false;
  if (getClass() != obj.getClass())
    return false;
 MyClass  other = (MyClass) obj;
  if (field1 == null) {
    if (other.field1 != null)
      return false;
  } else if (!field1.equals(other.field1))
    return false;
  if (field2 == null) {
    if (other.field2 != null)
      return false;
  } else if (!field2.equals(other.field2))
    return false;
  return true;
}
```

Unless your IDE can be configured to produce clean methods (as discussed below) we do not generally recommend this approach. It is easy for bugs to be introduced into this code by hand editing over time.

Hand Roll Clean Methods

Java 7 introduced the `java.util.Objects` class that makes implementing `hashCode` trivial. Guava provides the similar `com.google.common.base.Objects` class which may be used with earlier versions of Java.

```
@Override
public int hashCode() {
  return Objects.hash(field1, field2);
}
```

The `Objects` class also simplifies implementing equals a little by pushing most null checks into the `Objects.equals` method.

```
@Override
public boolean equals(Object obj) {
  if (this == obj) // <- performance optimisation
    return true;
  if (obj == null)
    return false;
  if (getClass() != obj.getClass()) // <- see note on inheritance
    return false;
  MyClass other = (MyClass) obj;
  return Objects.equals(field1, other.field1) &&
      Objects.equals(field2, other.field2);
}
```

The first `if` statement is not logically required and could be safely omitted; it may, however, provide performance benefits.

Usually, we would recommend that such micro-optimizations are not included unless they have been proven to provide a benefit. In the case of equals methods, we suggest that the optimization is left in place. It is likely to justify itself in at least some of your classes and there is value in having all methods follow an identical template.

The example above uses `getClass` to check that objects are of the same type. An alternative is to use `instanceof` as follows

```
@Override
public boolean equals(Object obj) {
  if (this == obj)
    return true;
  if (obj == null)
    return false;
  if (!(obj instanceof MyClass)) // <- compare with instanceof
    return false;
  MyClass other = (MyClass) obj;
  return Objects.equals(field1, other.field1) &&
      Objects.equals(field2, other.field2);
}
```

This results in a behavioral difference - comparing instances of `MyClass` with its subclasses will return true with `instanceof` but false with `getClass`.

In Effective Java Josh Bloch argues in favor of `instanceof` as the `getClass` implementation violates a strict interpretation of the Liskov substitution principle.

However, if `instanceof` is used, it is easy for the symmetric property of the equals contract to be violated if a subclass overrides equals. i.e.:

```
MyClass a = new MyClass();
ExtendsMyClassWithCustomEqual b = new ExtendsMyClassWithCustomEqual();

a.equals(b) // true
b.equals(a) // false, a violation of symmetry
```

If you find yourself in a situation where you need to consider the nuances of whether subclasses are equal to their parents then we strongly suggest you reconsider your design.

Having to think about maintaining the equals contract in a class hierarchy is painful and you shouldn't need to put yourself, or your team, through this for normal server-side coding tasks.

In the majority of cases, if you think it makes sense for your class to implement `hashCode` and `equals` , we strongly suggest you make your class final so hierarchies do not need to be considered.

If you believe you have a case where it makes sense for subclasses to be treated as equivalent to their parent, use `instanceof` but ensure that the parent equals method is made final.

Avoid relationships that are more complex than this.

Commons EqualsBuilder and HashCodeBuilder

The Apache commons hashcode and equals builders were once a popular way of generating these methods. We do not recommend their use in new code as most of what they achieved is now provided by `java.util.Objects` without bringing in a 3rd party library, or by the Guava equivalent.

These classes do provide the option of a single line reflection based implementation.

```
public boolean equals(Object obj) {
  return EqualsBuilder.reflectionEquals(this, obj);
}


public int hashCode() {
  return HashCodeBuilder.reflectionHashCode(this);
}
```

The brevity of these implementations is attractive, but their performance is measurably poorer than others discussed so far. Good performance tests and regular profiling can help determine whether a poorly performing method genuinely leads to performance bottlenecks in your application. If you are confident that you would detect such adverse impacts then using these methods as initial placeholder implementations may be a reasonable approach. But in general we suggest you avoid them.

Code Generators

A number of projects exist that can auto-generate value objects at build-time. Two of the better known options are :

- Google auto
- Project Lombok

But many others are available.

Google Auto

Google *Auto* will create a subclass with the *obvious* implementation of an abstract class annotated with `@AutoValue` . This implementation will include functioning `hashcode` and `equals` methods.

```
import com.google.auto.value.AutoValue;


@AutoValue
abstract class Animal {
  static Animal create(String name, int numberOfLegs) {
    return new AutoValue_Animal(name, numberOfLegs);
  }

  Animal() {}

  abstract String name();
  abstract int numberOfLegs();
}
```

This is clearly far less effort than hand crafting a complete `Animal` class, but there are some downsides.

Some of the issues with code generators are discussed in "Consider Code Generators Carefully", which categorized them into *friction* and *surprise*.

Here, Google Auto introduces some *friction* as the code shown above will not compile within an IDE until the generator has run to produce the `AutoValue_Animal` class.

There is also some *surprise*.

Because it is a value, Animal would normally be implemented as a final class - but we have been forced to make it abstract. The team behind *Auto* recommend you add a package-private constructor to prevent other child classes being created.

Unlike normal Java, the order in which accessors are declared is important because it is used by the generator to define the order of the constructor parameters. Re-ordering the accessors can, therefore, have the surprising effect of introducing a bug.

Lombok

Lombok can also (amongst other things) generate full implementations of value objects.

It takes a different approach to Google auto.

Given an annotated class such as:

```
@Value
public class ValueExample {
  String name;
  @NonFinal int age;
  double score;
}
```

It will alter the class at build-time to produce an implementation along the lines of:

```
public final class ValueExample {
  private final String name;
  private int age;
  private final double score;

  public ValueExample(String name, int age, double score) {
    this.name = name;
    this.age = age;
    this.score = score;
   }

  public String getName() {
    return this.name;
  }

  public int getAge() {
    return this.age;
  }

  public double getScore() {
    return this.score;
  }

  public boolean equals(Object o) {
   // valid implementation of equality based on all fields
  }

  public int hashCode() {
   // valid hashcode implementation based on all fields
  }
```

While Google *Value* asks the programmer to provide a valid public API for a class, *Lombok* creates the public API based on a description of its internal state. The description is valid Java syntax but has a different meaning when interpreted by Lombok.

Lombok causes some friction. It is not practical to use *Lombok* without an IDE that understands it - code using the autogenerated api will appear to be invalid. An IDE plugin must be installed.

While it (arguably) introduces less friction than auto once the IDE plugin is installed, the behavior of *Lombok* is much more surprising. It is easy to explain what *Auto* does - it generates a class at build-time that implements an interface you define. It is much harder to predict or explain what *Lombok* will do.

Although *Lombok* requires the programmer to write less code than solutions such as *Auto*, it deviates further from normal Java.

If you consider using a code generator for Value classes, we would recommend you consider approaches such as *Auto* before *Lombok*.

To its credit *Lombok* does provide an escape route (see "Prefer reversible decisions") in the form of delombok which allows you to output the generated classes. These can then be used to replace the annotated originals.

Removing *Auto* is similarly straightforward - the generated classes can be checked into the source tree. The artificial abstract class/implementation split can then be removed via simple refactorings.

Do Not Re-Assign Parameters

Summary

Parameters to methods should never be re-assigned.

Detail

Reassigning to parameters makes code harder to understand and provides no meaningful advantage over creating a new variable.

If the method is large, it can be difficult to track the lifecycle of a parameter. Even within short methods, re-using parameters will cause problem. As the variable is being used to represent two separate concepts, it is often not possible to name it meaningfully.

If another variable of the same type as a parameter is needed, it should be declared locally.

Bad

```
public String foo(String currentStatus) {
  if ( someLogic() ) {
    currentStatus  = "FOO";
  }
  return currentStatus;
}
```

Better

```
public String foo(final String currentStatus) {
  String desiredStatus = currentStatus;
  if ( someLogic() ) {
    desiredStatus = "FOO";
  }

  return desiredStatus ;
}
```

Parameters may be declared final so that the reader can tell at a glance that its value will not change.

Limit Variables to the Smallest Possible Scope

Summary

Variables should be declared as late as possible so that they have the narrowest possible scope.

Details

Bad

```
public void foo(String value) {
    String calculatedValue;
    if (someCondition()) {
        calculatedValue = calculateStr(value);
        doSomethingWithValue(calculatedValue);
    }
}
```

Better

```
public void foo(String value) {
    if (someCondition()) {
        String calculatedValue = calculateStr(value);
        doSomethingWithValue(calculatedValue);
    }
}
```

Better still

```
public void foo(String value) {
    if (someCondition()) {
        doSomethingWithValue(calculateStr(value));
    }
}
```

Sometimes, assigning to well-named, temporary variables will result in more readable code than calling a method inline because it helps the reader follow the data and logical flow.

As a rule of thumb, if you are unable to come up with a name for a variable that does little more than mirror a method from which its value was retrieved, then the variable should be eliminated.

Prefer For-Each Loops to For Loops

Summary

Use `for each` loops in preference to indexed for loops.

Details

The `for each` loop introduced with Java 5 avoids the potential out-by-one errors of indexed for loops and is more concise than code using iterators.

Bad

```
public List<String> selectValues(List<Integer> someIntegers) {
  List<String> filteredStrings = new ArrayList<String>();
  for (int i = 0; i != someIntegers.size(); i++) {
    Integer value = someIntegers.get(i);
    if (value > 20) {
      filteredStrings.add(value.toString());
    }
  }
  return filteredStrings;
}
```

A little better

```
public List<String> selectValues(List<Integer> someIntegers) {
  List<String> filteredStrings = new ArrayList<String>();
  for (Integer value : someIntegers) {
    if (value > 20) {
      filteredStrings.add(value.toString());
    }
  }
  return filteredStrings;
}
```

Prefer Maps and Filters to Imperative Loops

Summary

Imperative loops hide application logic inside boilerplate code - prefer maps and filters as these separate the logic from the implementation.

Details

Most loop based code can be re-written in a more declarative style using filters and maps.

Java 8 made this easy by introducing lambdas and the streams API, but the same style can be applied in Java 7 using anonymous inner classes and third party libraries such as Guava.

Filters and maps highlight what the code is intended to achieve. This is less clear in the imperative implementation.

Bad

```
public List<String> selectValues(List<Integer> someIntegers) {
  List<String> filteredStrings = new ArrayList<String>();
  for (Integer value : someIntegers) {
    if (value > 20) {
      filteredStrings.add(value.toString());
    }
  }
  return filteredStrings;
}
```

Better (Java 8)

```
public List<String> selectValues(List<Integer> someIntegers) {
  return someIntegers.stream()
      .filter(i -> i > 20)
      .map(i -> i.toString())
      .collect(Collectors.toList());
}
```

Better (Java 7 using Guava)

```
public List<String> selectValues(List<Integer> someIntegers) {
  return FluentIterable
  .from(someIntegers)
  .filter(greaterThan(20))
  .transform(Functions.toStringFunction())
  .toList();
}

private static Predicate<Integer> greaterThan(final int limit) {
  return new Predicate<Integer>() {
    @Override
    public boolean apply(Integer input) {
      return input > limit;
    }
  };
}
```

Note that, although the Java 7 version requires more lines of code (in the form of the ugly boilerplate for the anonymous inner class), the logic of the `selectValues` method is clearer. If the logic required in the Predicate or mapping Function is required in multiple places then it is straightforward to move this to a common location. This is harder to achieve with the imperative version.

Also note that the method that creates the Predicate has been made static. It is a good idea to do this, where possible, when returning an anonymous class to prevent a long lived instance preventing the parent class from being garbage collected. Although the Predicate is only short-lived in this instance, applying static dogmatically in all cases avoids the overhead of thinking.

Avoid APIs from Pre-History

Summary

Do not use `Vector` , `StringBuffer` and other archaic parts of the JDK.

Details

Java has been around for over 20 years. In order to maintain backwards compatibility, it has hoarded all manner of APIs that no longer make sense to use. Some of them are handily marked with @Deprecated annotation, others are not.

Unfortunately, many are still used in university courses and online examples. New Java programmers may not be aware they have been replaced - a few to watch out for include:

- `java.util.Vector` - use `ArrayList` instead
- `java.lang.StringBuffer` - use `StringBuilder` instead
- `java.util.Stack` - use a `Dequeue` (e.g. `ArrayDeqeue`)
- `java.util.Hashtable` - use a `Map` (e.g. `HashMap`)
- `java.util.Enumeration` - use an `Iterator` or an `Iterable`

Each of these replacements (except `Enumeration`) differ from the originals by not being synchronized. If you think you need a synchronized collection go away somewhere quiet and think again.

Beware Casts and Generics Warnings

Summary

Casts dilute the benefit of Java's type system, making code both less readable and less safe.

Avoid casts wherever possible.

If you find yourself writing one, stop and ask yourself why you are writing it.

What would need to be changed in your code so you did not need to write that cast?

Why can't you make that change?

Detail

Java's type system is there to help us - it catches bugs at compile-time and documents our code, making it easier to understand and navigate.

When we add a cast to our code, we lose both these benefits.

Casts get introduced into code for three main reasons:

1. We have reached the limits of Java's type system and the programmer must take control
2. The overall design of the code is poor
3. The code uses raw generic types

We'll look at these in reverse order.

Code with Raw Types

If code contains raw generic types (either because the code pre-dates Java 5 or the programmer is not familiar with Java) then it will create the need to cast.

For example:

```
List list = numberList();
for (Object each : list) {
  Integer i = (Integer) each;
  // do things with integers
}
```

The compiler will not be happy that we have failed to fully declare the type of `List` we are dealing with and will (depending on how it's been configured) generate an error or warning on the line where `list` is declared e.g.

```
List is a raw type. References to generic type List<E> should be parameterized
```

Similarly, for errant code such as:

```
List l = new ArrayList<Number>();
List<String> ls = l;
```

The compiler will issue:

```
The expression of type List needs unchecked conversion to conform to List<String>
```

Make sure that all such warnings are addressed, either by imposing a zero compiler warnings policy or by configuring the compiler to treat them as errors.

In this case, removing both the cast and the warning is straight forward:

```
List<Integer> list = numberList();
for (Integer each : list) {
   // do things with each
}
```

Poor Design

Sometimes, removing a cast or fixing a warning is non-trivial. We have bumped into issue two - poor design.

For example:

```
List<Widget> widgets = getWidgets();
List results = process(widgets);

for (Object each : results) {
  if (each instanceof String) {
    // handle failure using data from string
  } else {
    EnhancedWidget widget = (EnhancedWidget) each;
    widget.doSomething();
  }
}
```

Normally, objects placed into a collection should be of a single type or of multiple types related by a common superclass or interface.

Here, unrelated types have been placed into the same list with a String used to communicate some sort of information about how "processing" of a widget has failed.

The classic OO fix for this code would be to introduce a `ProcessResult` interface with two concrete implementations.

```
interface ProcessResult {
 void doSomething();
}

class Success implements ProcessResult {

  private final EnhancedWidget result;

  @Override
  public void doSomething() {
    result.doSomething();
  }

}

class Failure implements ProcessResult {

  private final String result;

  @Override
  public void doSomething() {
    // do something with result string
  }

}
```

The original code can then be fixed as follows:

```
List<Widget> widgets = getWidgets();
List<ProcessResult> results = process(widgets);

for (ProcessResult each : results) {
    each.doSomething();
  }
}
```

Or, more concisely in Java 8:

```
List<ProcessResult> results = process(widgets);
results.stream().forEach(ProcessResult::doSomething);
```

It may also sometimes make sense to use a disjoint union type aka `Either` .

This technique can be particularly useful as an interim step when reworking legacy code that uses mixed type raw collections, but can also be a sensible approach when dealing with error conditions.

Unfortunately, Java does not provide an `Either` type out of the box but at its simplest it looks something like:

```
public class Either<L,R> {
  private final L left;
  private final R right;

  private Either(L left, R right) {
    this.left = left;
    this.right = right;
  }

  public static <L, R> Either<L, R> left(final L left) {
    return new Either<L, R>(left,null);
  }

  public static <L, R> Either<L, R> right(final R right) {
    return new Either<L, R>(null,right);
  }

  boolean isLeft() {
    return left != null;
  }

  L left() {
    return left;
  }

  R right() {
    return right;
  }

}
```

Libraries such as Atlassian's Fugue provide implementations with much richer functionality.

Using the simplistic form of `Either` with Java 7 the code could be re-written as:

```
List<Widget> widgets = getWidgets();
List<Either<ProcessResult,String>> results = process(widgets);

for (Either<ProcessResult,String> each : results) {
  if (each.isLeft()) {
    // handle failure using data from string
  } else {
    each.right().doSomething();
  }
}
```

While most Java programmers will prefer the earlier OO version, this version has two advantages:

1. It requires no change to the *structure* of the original code - all we have really done is make the types document what is happening
2. It requires less code

This pattern can help quickly tame a legacy code base that is difficult to comprehend.

Limits of the Type System

Sometimes we do reach the limits of Java's type system and need to cast.

Before we do this, we must make certain that the cast is safe and there is no better solution to our problem.

Similarly, we may need to sometimes suppress a Generics warning, this can be done by annotating with `@SuppressWarnings` e.g.

```
@SuppressWarnings("unchecked")
<T> T read(final Class<T> type, String xml) {
  return (T) fromXml(xml);
}

Object fromXml(final String xml) {
  return ... // de-serialise from string
}
```

Here, the compiler has no way of knowing what type has been serialized to the String. Hopefully the programmer does or else a runtime error will occur.

Do Not Use Magic Numbers

Summary

Magic numbers should be replaced with well-named constants that describe their meaning.

Detail

Placing numeric or string literals directly into source code causes two problems:

1. It is unlikely that the **meaning** of the literal will be clear
2. If the value changes updates are required where ever the literal has been duplicated

Literals should therefore be replaced with well-named constants and Enums.

Bad

```
public void fnord(int i) {
  if (i == 1) {
    performSideEffect();
  }
}
```

Better

```
public void fnord(int i) {
  if (i == VALID) {
    performSideEffect();
  }
}
```

You've missed the point

```
public void fnord(int i) {
  if (i == ONE) {
    performSideEffect();
  }
}
```

If the constants you extract relate to an identifiable concept, create an Enum instead:

Good

```
public void fnord(FnordStatus status) {
  if (status == FnordStatus.VALID) {
    performSideEffect();
  }
}
```

Some coding standards make statements such as "0 and 1 are exceptions to this rule". This is, however, an oversimplification.

Sometimes 0 and 1 will have a clear local meaning as they are being used as part of low level code e.g.:

```
if (list.size() == 0) {...}
```

But 0 and 1 may also have domain-specific values that should be extracted into constants like any other literal.

Server-side Java can also often be re-written in a cleaner fashion without the use of numeric literals, e.g.:

```
if (list.isEmpty()) {...}
```

Don't Use the Assert Keyword

Summary

Assertions are a useful coding technique that can provide many benefits but in most circumstances it is better to implement them using third party libraries rather than the `assert` keyword.

Details

Assertions written with the assert keyword are only enabled when the `-ea` JVM flag is set.

The intent of this flag is to allow the assertions to be enabled in development and testing but disabled in production to avoid the performance overhead of assertion logic. This is usually a premature optimization and increases the opportunity for mistakes as the code will behave differently in development vs production.

Switching off assertions in production also greatly dilutes their value. If a coding error has been made assertions ensure that it is reported early, close to the bug. If assertions are turned off in production bugs may propagate silently. This may make their consequences more severe and will certainly make the issue harder to diagnose.

So for these reasons, unless you are working in a very performance sensitive domain, assertions should always be enabled.

For always-on assertions third party libraries such as Guava's preconditions provide a better solution than the `assert` keyword.

A separate issue is the use of the `assert` keyword in tests. This is usually the result of a lack of familiarity with Java and JUnit.

In codebases found in the wild where `assert` has been used in tests the `-ea` flag is rarely set, meaning that the tests can never fail. For tests JUnit's built in assertions or modern test focused assertion libraries such as AssertJ should always be used.

Avoid Floats and Doubles

Summary

Avoid using floats and doubles (both the primitives and their wrappers).

Detail

Floats and doubles introduce a minefield of rounding and comparison issues. While they are a sensible choice for some domains where you do not care about rounding errors integers or `BigDecimal` are usually a better choice for server-side business code.

The core issue is that floating point numbers are not able to represent many numbers (e.g. `0.1`).

This leads to unexpected results that may not be caught by simple test cases

```
double balance = 2.00;
double transationCost = 0.10;
int numberTransactions = 6;

System.out.printf("After %s transactions balance is %s"
                , numberTransactions
                , balance - (transationCost * numberTransactions));
// Gives After 6 transactions balance is 1.4 :-)
```

But

```
double balance = 2.00;
double transationCost = 0.10;
int numberTransactions = 7;

System.out.printf("After %s transactions balance is %s"
                 , numberTransactions
                 , balance - (transationCost * numberTransactions));
// Gives After 7 transactions balance is 1.2999999999999998 :-(
```

The simplest solution in this case would be to replace the floats with integer values (i.e. track the balance in units of cents rather than dollars).

In situations where floats can't be replaced by integers code can be re-written to use `BigDecimal` .

```
BigDecimal balance = new BigDecimal("2.00");
BigDecimal transationCost = new BigDecimal("0.10");

BigDecimal numberTransactions = BigDecimal.valueOf(7);

System.out.printf("After %s transactions balance is %s"
                  , numberTransactions
                  , balance.subtract(transationCost.multiply(numberTransactions)));

// Gives After 7 transactions balance is 1.30 :-)
```

Note that although `BigDecimal` can be constructed from a float this would take us back to where we started.

```
BigDecimal balance = new BigDecimal("2.00");
BigDecimal transationCost = new BigDecimal(0.10); // <- float used to construct

BigDecimal numberTransactions = BigDecimal.valueOf(7);

System.out.printf("After %s transactions balance is %s"
                  , numberTransactions
                  , balance.subtract(transationCost.multiply(numberTransactions)));

// Gives After 7 transactions
// balance is 1.2999999999999999611421941381195210851728916168212890625
```

When to use floats and doubles

Floats and doubles clearly can't be all bad or it is unlikely that they would have been included in the Java language.

The primitive floating point types have performance advantages over `BigDecimal` that can be significant in highly numerical domains such as machine learning, physics engines, scientific applications etc. In these domains the performance benefit may greatly out-weigh the additional risk of error.

Code using `BigDecimal` is also inherently more verbose and clumsy than code that uses primitives. If you are working in a domain where the imprecision of floating point types is acceptable you might prefer the cleaner code they allow, but be sure you are making this choice consciously with an understanding of the pitfalls involved.

Don't use Reflection

Summary

Do not use reflection in your code (i.e. anything from the `java.lang.reflect` package).

Details

Reflection is a powerful tool; it allows Java to do things that would otherwise be either impossible or require large amounts of boilerplate code.

But, while it is sometimes useful when creating a framework or library it is unlikely to be a good way to solve the types of problem we encounter in normal server-side application code.

So why would we want to avoid using a powerful tool that Java provides?

Reflection has three main drawbacks:

Loss of Compile Time Safety

Reflection moves errors from compile time to runtime - this is a Bad Thing ™

The compiler is our first form of defense against defects and the type system is one of the most effective tools we have to document our code. We should not throw these things away lightly.

Loss of Refactor Safety

Refactoring and code analysis tools are blind to reflection.

Although they may make some attempt to take it into account, the additional possibilities reflection creates for how a program might behave means the tools can no longer provide rigorous guarantees that they have understood the program. In the presence of reflection refactorings that would otherwise be safe may change program and analysis tools may report incorrect results.

Harder Code Comprehension

In the same way that Reflection makes it harder for automated tools to understand code, it also makes it harder for humans to understand code.

Reflection introduces surprises.

This method is never called, I can safely delete it. Oh. Reflection.

I can safely change the behavior of this private method as I know where it is called from. Oh. Reflection.

Good Tests

The testing pyramid and different levels of tests are discussed in "Agree the language you use for tests".

As discussed in that section it is important to maintain a layered strategy with many fast running unit tests and smaller numbers of integration and system tests. The precise proportions that work best will vary from project to project but the pyramid formation will hold.

Although it is important to write tests at all these levels this section mainly concerns itself with unit tests as these are the ones we write most of and run most frequently.

Write Specifications Not Tests

Before you sit down to write a test it's important to understand *why* you are doing it.

What is it that you want to achieve?

There is an unfortunate tendency for developers to look at tests as a thing you have to do because it's "best practice". Some extra work to be performed after the real work is done. A chore.

The reason for writing them has become lost.

Why Write Tests?

The reason to write tests is to make our lives easier.

If we are not writing tests that do this we should stop writing them.

A good test should do all of the following:

- Enable refactoring by preventing regression when the implementation changes
- Catch bugs during initial coding
- Document how the code behaves
- Inform the design of the code

When tests are viewed as a chore to be completed after the code is written only this first point is considered.

Often it is not achieved.

Tests written with this mindset can have a negative value:

- Instead of enabling refactoring they can increase its cost.
- Instead of documenting what the code does, the tests are harder to understand than the code itself.
- Instead of aiding development they increase the work that must be done

This first problem causes the most pain.

If you have a test that is tied to the code's implementation, to change the way the code is implemented you have to spend effort changing the test.

If the test must change whenever the implementation changes then we cannot trust that the test will stop regression. How do we know we did not introduce a bug into the test when we changed it?

Executable Specifications

So how do we make sure we do not write negative value tests? How do we make sure we write tests that provide the benefits in our list?

The first thing to do is let go of the idea that we are testing.

We are not testing, we're *specifying*.

To test something you only need to verify that it "does what it does". To specify you need to describe the important things that it must do in a way that can be clearly understood.

A good specification describes *only* the important things.

It describes what something *must* do without making assumptions about how it will do it. It allows for multiple implementations. If a specification is tied to one implementation then it is *over-specified* and will have to change when the implementation does.

So this is what we must aim for - an executable specification of our code.

Unfortunately it is very hard to do.

Specification First

One simple technique that can help is to write the specification before the code. i.e. TDD.

A rigorous TDD cycle proceeds in very small steps.

First write a test and run it to ensure that it fails.

Next write just enough code to make that test pass (and no more).

Take a moment to see if there is a sensible refactoring that would improve the code, then write the next test and continue the cycle.

This has several advantages:

- It guarantees that all the code *can* be tested
- As there is no implementation when the test is written it is harder to write a test that is tied to one
- It guarantees that all behavior is covered by tests
- It discourages writing superfluous code

There are two important aspects to TDD:

1. Writing the specification first
2. Moving in very small steps

Both of these practices are a good idea individually, even if they are not combined.

If we wrote our specification first, but moved in larger steps (possibly because we believed we knew what our implementation should look like) we would realize our first advantage - a guarantee that the code we wrote could be tested.

What do we mean by this?

If code is not written with testing in mind then it can be difficult to write a test for it that fits our definition of a *unit* test.

We can make our code more likely to be testable by following simple rules such as:

- Always inject dependencies
- Avoid global state (singletons, static variables, ThreadLocals, registries etc)

But even if we follow these rules we can still find that it is difficult to test our code if we have not designed for it. Writing our specification first requires our design to consider testing.

Although we ensured our code was testable, because we moved in large steps with an implementation in mind we might not achieve the other benefits.

If we were to write our code without first writing a test we might discover we were finished that our code was difficult to test. The process of writing that code would however have been easier if we had applied the second technique - moving in small steps.

If we wrote only a small amount of code before executing it and observing the result of each small code change, we would probably spend less time debugging, be less likely to write code we did not need and move faster over all.

TDD has many advantages but it is not magic.

Even if it is applied rigorously it is entirely possible to write terrible code and specifications. TDD doesn't mean you can stop thinking.

Despite this, if you have a good understanding of the technologies and domain in which you are working, TDD is usually the best approach if you wish to optimize for quality.

If you do not understand your domain or technology well you may find writing a specification first hard.

The classic solution to this problem is to first gain understanding by producing a throw away spike.

Spikes

A spike is just some quick and dirty code to explore how you might tackle the problem. At the end of the spike you will know if that approach works well or if it is worth looking for alternative approaches.

By producing a spike, you gain more understanding of both the domain and the technology you are working with. Even if the conclusion at the end of the spike is that it was a poor approach, the spike was still useful as it increased your understanding.

Once you have learned what you can from the spike, it should be thrown away and the final code test driven using the knowledge you have gained.

Spike and Stabilize

Traditionally, spikes are thrown away as they are inherently of low quality. Discarding the spike is done to optimize code quality at the expense of a (probably) slower delivery.

Sometimes this is not the trade-off you want.

An alternative is to try to stabilize the spike so that it is fit for use. If you do this, you will usually end up with something of lower quality than if you had started again.

You will also end up spending more effort on this piece of code over the lifetime of the project than if you had thrown the spike away.

What you gain for this loss in quality and increase in effort is a faster *first* delivery. Sometimes this is a trade-off worth making, sometimes it is not.

Think Units, Not Methods

Each behavior that a unit test describes should normally relate to the overall *unit* rather than the responsibilities of an individual method.

What is a Unit?

To think in terms of units we have to first answer the difficult question of what a *unit* actually is.

Testing in terms of methods is effectively the same as saying that a *unit* is a method. It is easy to show why this does not always work.

If we were to try and write a unit test for the `push` method of `java.util.Stack` we might end up with something like:

```
@Test
public void testPush() {
   Stack<String> testee = new Stack<String>();
   testee.push("foo");
   assertThat(testee.pop()).isEqualTo("foo");
};
```

Now lets test the `pop` method:

```
@Test
public void testPop() {
   Stack<String> testee = new Stack<String>();
   testee.push("foo");
   assertThat(testee.pop()).isEqualTo("foo");
};
```

Oh. That looks familiar.

The problem we are hitting is that we have defined too small a *unit*. We are trying to describe the behavior of something that is only useful when it collaborates with other *units* of the same size.

If we start thinking of `java.util.Stack` as our *unit* then tests become much easier to write:

```
@Test
public void shouldRetrieveValuesInOrderTheyAreAdded() {
  Stack<String> testee = new Stack<String>();
  testee.push("a");
  testee.push("b");
  assertThat(testee.pop()).isEqualTo("b");
  assertThat(testee.pop()).isEqualTo("a");
}
```

We have written a test that, instead of trying to describe what a method does, describes the behavior of the class as a whole.

The idea that our job is to test methods is common with developers that are new to unit testing, and is unfortunately re-enforced by some IDEs and tools that provide templates to generate tests for each method of a class.

As we have seen, for `Stack` it makes far more sense to consider the behavior of the class of a whole.

Are Classes Units?

It often does make sense to treat a class as a *unit* so this is a good default definition, but it isn't always the right granularity.

If we were to try to test the `java.util.Collections` class we would find that it is perfectly reasonable to treat the `sort` , `reverse` , `singleton` , etc. methods as separate *units*. Each one represents a self contained logical behavior.

So sometimes *units* are as small as methods.

Sometimes they are also larger than a single class.

If we were to inherit the code below without any tests what tests might we write for it?

```
public class ThingaMeBob {

  private final Iterable<MatchingBinaryOperator> actions;

  ThingaMeBob() {
    actions = Arrays.asList(new Addition(), new Subtraction());
  }

  public int process(String s, int a, int b) {
    for (MatchingBinaryOperator each : actions) {
      if (each.match(s)) {
        return each.apply(a,b);
      }
    }

    throw new RuntimeException();
  }

}

class Addition implements MatchingBinaryOperator {
  public boolean match(String s) {
    return "add".equals(s);
  }
  public int apply(int a, int b) {
    return a + b;
  }
}

class Subtraction implements MatchingBinaryOperator {
  public boolean match(String s) {
    return "minus".equals(s);
  }
  public int apply(int a, int b) {
    return a - b;
  }
}
```

We might write tests for the Addition and Subtraction classes:

```
public class AdditionTest {

  Addition testee = new Addition();

  @Test
  public void shouldMatchWhenStringIsAdd() {
  }

  @Test
  public void shouldNotMatchWhenStringIsNotAdd() {
  }

  @Test
  public void shouldAddTwoNumbers() {
  }

  // etc

}
```

And for the `ThingaMeBob` class:

```
public class ThingaMeBobTest {

  ThingaMeBob testee = new ThingaMeBob();

  @Test
  public void shouldAddTwoNumbers() {
  }

  @Test
  public void shouldSubtractTwoNumbers() {
  }

  // etc

}
```

At some point we would hopefully question why this code is so over-engineered and consider refactoring to something simpler like.

```
public class ThingaMeBob {

  public int process(String s, int a, int b) {
    if ("add".equals(s)) {
      return a + b;
    }

    if ("minus".equals(s)) {
      return a - b;
    }

    throw new RuntimeException();
  }

}
```

What happens to our tests?

Which ones were most valuable?

The answer of course is that the test which exercised all three classes through the public interface of `ThingaMeBob` proved the most useful. We did not have to change it at all. When it ran green we knew our refactoring was successful and everything still works.

We deleted the ones for `Addition` and `Subtraction` . The smaller units we created were just implementation detail.

Lets re-wind and imagine things happened differently.

What if we were asked to test drive the desired behavior from scratch? What would we write?

We would most likely write something that looked like our 2nd simpler version of `ThingaMeBob` and a test that looked something like `ThingAMeBobTest` .

If we were then asked to add support for another 10 operations, we might leave our design fundamentally the same.

What if a new requirement came for the behavior in `ThingAMeBob` to be more dynamic, with different operations being enabled and disabled at runtime?

It would then make sense to refactor to something like our earlier more complex version.

What should we do with the tests?

We would already have tests written in terms of `ThingaMeBob` that describe all supported behaviors. Should we also fully describe `Addition` , `Subtraction` and the other 10 operations with tests as we extract them into classes?

There is no right answer here, but I hope it is clear that the most useful *unit* that we have identified is `ThingaMeBob` . The smaller *units* are part of just one implementation of the functionality we require.

If we choose to write tests for each extracted class those tests would have some value.

The test written in terms of `ThingaMeBob` would do a poor job of describing what each of the small extracted units does. If a test was failing it wouldn't be instantly obvious which class the bug was in. If we had to change one of the extracted classes it wouldn't be instantly obvious which test to run.

So there is definitely value in writing tests for each of the extracted classes. At the same time, if we were not to do so, that would also be a reasonable decision and it would reduce the cost of the refactoring.

The `ThingaMeBob` tests will be fast and repeatable and allow us to work easily with the code. If we could only have tests at one level, the level we would choose is `ThingaMeBob` .

So, as a starting point, assume that a *unit* will be a class, but recognize that this is not a hard rule.

A *unit* is really a "single self contained logical concern" - it may make sense to have several classes collaborate in order to capture that concern - as long as that collaboration provides a single well defined entry point.

Making units too small may be a form of over-specifying.

Making units too large may result in tests that are difficult to understand and expensive to maintain.

As a rule of thumb, if you might reasonably have made one or more classes inner classes of a different class, perhaps they should be treated as a single unit.

Name Test Cases With a Specification Style

Use the name of each test case to describe one (and **only** one) behavior of the unit under test. The name should be a proposition - i.e. a statement that could be true or false.

The method name should start with *should*.

This is superfluous once you get good at writing test names, but in a mixed team it is useful as it encourages thinking about the test in the right way.

The rest of the name should describe a behavior and, optionally, a scenario (identified by the word When).

For example, we might start to describe `java.util.Stack` with:

- `shouldBeEmptyWhenCreated`
- `shouldReturnItemsInOrderTheyWereAdded`
- `shouldThrowAnErrorWhenItemsRemovedFromEmptyStack`

Contrast this with common naming patterns found in some code bases:

- `emptyStack`
- `testEmptyStack`
- `testPush`

These names alone tell us nothing about how a `Stack` should behave.

If we omit *should* we can create more concise names

- `isEmptyWhenCreated`
- `returnsItemsInOrderTheyAreAdded`
- `throwsAnErrorWhenItemsRemovedFromEmptyStack`

Although more verbose the formulaic *should* form has an advantage - it provides a clear pattern to follow.

If a developer knows that a test name must start with *should* (often because they have seen this pattern within existing tests) it is hard for them to revert to a different style and write a test that is not a proposition.

The verbosity of *should* pays for itself by forcing developers to think about tests in the right fashion.

Kevlin Henney compares *shoulds* to training wheels on a bike - a device to help while we are learning.

So when should we take the training wheels off?

This depends on the makeup of the team and how often the team changes.

If the majority of people who are likely to work on the codebase over its lifetime are accustomed to writing tests in this style then the added verbosity is not worth it. If a sufficiently large proportion are not then it is probably best for the team to stick with the convention.

Use the Example Style When Specification Style Does Not Work

Occasionally, it is not possible to follow the specification naming style because the descriptions become too long and unwieldy. If it feels like your method names are becoming overly long ask yourself two questions:

1. Am I really testing only one thing?
2. Is my unit doing too much?

If you're confident the answer is "no" to both then switch to a different style - example style.

In example style the name describes only the "When" part. It does not describe the expected behavior, e.g.:

- `emptyStack`
- `oneItemAdded`
- `removalFromEmptyStack`

To understand tests named with the example style, you must read the code within the tests. For this reason, this specification style should be preferred when possible.

Avoid Method Names in Test Descriptions Where Possible

Where possible, avoid including method names in test names.

On a practical level this avoids the extra overhead of updating test names if method names are ever refactored.

More subtly, including names can make you think in the wrong fashion - verifying method implementation rather than specifying unit behavior.

This is not a hard rule - sometimes it will be difficult or impossible to describe a meaningful behavior without referring to the unit's interface.

The domain language may also overlap with the method names, so you may find yourself using the same **words** as are also used as a method name.

Pick Examples Carefully

Traditional testing is performed with examples.

The overall behavior of the component or unit is explained by supplying a series of example input and output values, or example interactions with other components.

Our goal is to use examples to

- Communicate the general expected behavior
- Communicate the behavior at any edge cases
- Gain confidence that our code is correct and remains correct when we change it

So how should we pick these examples?

One approach is to look at the possible inputs to the component under test.

We could fully specify our code if we provided the expected output for each possible input. Usually, this is not practical because the possible range of inputs is far too large. Instead, we can look for categories of values within the possible range of inputs (e.g *valid* and *invalid*) and pick an example from each one.

However, the best approach is usually not to think in terms of possible inputs and examples, but to instead think first of the behaviors we would like our code to exhibit.

Once we have identified the behavior we can then pick examples that demonstrate it. The actual values used are often unimportant - "Make tests easy to understand" discusses some techniques to make unimportant values less prominent in tests and highlight the important ones.

Property-based testing takes this a stage further.

Properties are identified that must hold true for all inputs or for a subset of possible inputs that meet certain criteria. The tests do not contain any example values - just a description of how they must be constrained. The examples used to check the properties are generated randomly and only ever seen if the check fails.

There are some compelling advantages to property based testing:

- The tests describe what is important about the input values. In example testing this must be inferred by the reader
- The tests will automatically find edge cases and bad assumptions made by the programmer

There is currently little experience with property-based testing in the Java community, so questions remain on how best to use it.

One obvious issue is that it introduces randomness, although most frameworks provide some mechanism to control it and repeat test runs.

Follow the Zero, One and Many Rule

If your components deals with numbers or collections of things, make sure you use sufficient examples to describe its behavior.

A good rule thumb is that test cases covering 0 (or empty), 1 and "many" are likely to be necessary. There will also be important edge cases, e.g. algorithmic code dealing with integers might need to consider `Integer.MAX` and `Integer.MIN` .

The zero, one many rule defines the minimum number of cases you can hope to consider. To properly describe your code's behavior will likely require many more.

When test driving, it is usually easiest to start with the *zero* test case.

Test One Thing at a Time

Each test case should specify one thing and one thing only.

Multiple assertions within a test may be an indicator that the test is testing more than one thing. Multiple assertions should be treated with suspicion, but are not necessarily a problem e.g.

```
@Test
public void shouldReturnItemsInOrderTheyWereAdded() {
   ArrayDeque<String> testee = new ArrayDeque<String>();

   testee.add("foo");
   testee.add("bar");

   assertEquals("foo",testee.pop());
   assertEquals("bar",testee.pop());
}
```

This test tests only one concern, but uses multiple asserts to do so.

Test Each Thing Only Once

Once you've tested a concern, don't let it leak into other tests - if you do then those tests are no longer testing only one thing.

This is a particularly easy mistake to make with interaction-based testing. If it is vitally important that the method `anImportantSideEffect` is called, it is easy to find yourself verifying that method in each test case.

If the contract ever changes so that this side effect is not longer important, all tests will need to be updated.

This concern should instead by covered by a single test case `shouldPerformImportantSideEffect` .

Although we shouldn't let a property leak into test cases where it does not belong this does not necessarily mean that it will be confined to a single test case. It may take several examples to fully demonstrate a property.

Make Tests Easy to Understand

One of our goals when writing a test is to document what the code under tests does.

We achieve this in part by choosing clear specification style names for each test case, but we must also ensure that the code implementing each test case is easy to understand.

Some techniques that help achieve this are discussed below.

Make Test Structure Clear

A test can be viewed as having three parts:

- Given - create the values and objects required for the test
- When - executes the code under test
- Then - verifies the output/behavior is as expected

These stages are also sometimes called *arrange*, *act* and *assert* by people particularly attached to the letter 'a'.

Although it is important that these three stages are visible, trying to rigorously separate them or label them with comments adds noise to a test.

Bad

```
@Test
public void shouldRetrieveValuesInOrderTheyAreAdded() {

  // given
  Stack<String> testee = new Stack<String>();
  String expectedFirstValue = "a";
  String expectedSecondValue = "b";

  // when
  testee.push(expectedFirstValue);
  testee.push(expectedSecondValue);
  String actualFirstValue = testee.pop();
  String actualSecondValue = testee.pop();

  // then
  assertThat(actualFirstValue).isEqualTo(secondValue);
  assertThat(actualSecondValue).isEqualTo(firstValue);
}
```

Better

```
@Test
public void shouldRetrieveValuesInOrderTheyAreAdded() {
  Stack<String> testee = new Stack<String>();
  testee.push("a");
  testee.push("b");
  assertThat(testee.pop()).isEqualTo("b");
  assertThat(testee.pop()).isEqualTo("a");
}
```

Follow Standard TEA Naming Convention for Test Variables

Establishing simple conventions can make some very basic things about a test clear to a reader.

If the unit you are testing is a class make this clear by always naming it `testee` within a test.

If you need to store an expected value in a variable, call it `expected` (but don't store it in a variable just for the sake of it).

If you need to store a result that you will compare against an expected value in variable, name it `actual` (but don't store it in a variable just for the sake of it).

If you have stubbed a participant consider naming it `stubbedFoo` , if it is acting as a mock name it `mockedFoo` . This rule is less hard than the others - decide on a case by case basis whether you think it makes your test more or less readable.

Highlight What is Important, Hide What is Not

It should be possible to read each test case at a glance - so make things clear by highlighting what is important for that test case and hiding what is not.

If an aspect of the input is important to the test case, highlight it by setting it **explicitly** in the test case - don't rely on that value being set in a generic setup method.

Even if the same value is set by default, it is better to re-supply it in the test so it is clearly visible.

If a particular value is not important, indicate this to the reader by using well-known neutral values such as `"foo"` for strings, or use clear names such as `someInt` or `anInt` for variables and methods that supply values.

Supplying values via a method call makes them less visible.

What is important in the test below?

Bad

```
@Test
public void shouldXXX() {
  MyClass testee = new MyClass();
  assertThat(testee.process(0, "", 3))
    .isEqualTo(Status.FAIL);
}
```

How about this version?

Better

```
@Test
public void shouldXXX() {
  int invalidValue = 3;
  MyClass testee = new MyClass();
  assertThat(testee.process(anInt(), aString(), invalidValue))
    .isEqualTo(Status.FAIL);
}
```

While we need additional context to understand why `3` is an invalid value, it should be clear that the first two parameters to the `process` method are not important to the behavior we are specifying.

Why is it important that the testee below returns the enum `CONTINUE` ?

Bad

```
@Test
public void shouldXXX() {
  assertThat(testee.process()).isEqualTo(CONTINUE);
}
```

If we look through the rest of the class we might find:

```
@Before
public void setup() {
   MyClass testee = new MyClass();
   testee.setDefaultProcessState(CONTINUE);
}
```

Other tests might not need to care about what the default state is, but this test does so we should write:

Better

```
@Test
public void shouldXXX() {
  testee.setDefaultProcessState(CONTINUE);
  assertThat(testee.process()).isEqualTo(CONTINUE);
}
```

As we start to deal with more complex domain objects, it becomes harder to separate the important values from the ones that are required to construct valid objects but not of particular interest to our test. Fortunately, we can use the builder pattern to ease the pain, reduce duplication, and keep the tests readable.

Name Values Meaningfully

If a value has an important meaning, make that meaning clear e.g.:

```
Foo testee = new Foo(PERFORM_VALIDATION);
```

instead of:

```
Foo testee = new Foo(true);
```

Write DAMP Test Code

As we have seen, in order to highlight that a value is important to a test, we need to keep it within the test method that uses it. This may introduce duplication which we might not accept in normal code - but test code is a little different.

Copy and paste coding is bad in tests as well as production code - the more code there is, the harder it is to read and a change to a concern will result in shotgun surgery if it has been duplicated throughout the tests.

Repetition should therefore generally be avoided in test code.

Test code **is** different from production code however.

Test code must tell more of a story - highlighting what is important and hiding what is not. Test code should not be as DRY (**D**on't **R**epeat **Y**ourself) as production code. It should be DAMP (contain **D**escriptive **A**nd **M**eaningful **P**hrases).

If refactoring a small amount of code out of a test method into a shared method hides what is happening, accept the duplication and leave it in place. If it does not affect readability then refactor mercilessly.

Choose the Right Assertion Method

When a test fails, a good assertion tells you what is wrong.

Although JUnit allows you to supply an assertion message this adds noise to the test. Like comments, these messages should be saved for those occasions when you cannot communicate using code alone.

Bad

```
assertTrue("Expected 2 but got " + actual, actual == 2);
```

Good

```
assertEquals(2, actual);
```

The built in assertions are fairly limited. Alternative assertion libraries such as AssertJ provide richer functionality and result in more readable code.

Understand How to Use Mocks and Stubs

There are two sorts of code and they require two different sorts of test.

Worker code does stuff. We can test worker code with **state based testing** - i.e. asserting that expected values are returned from methods, or objects are left in expected states.

State based testing is easily recognized as it will use assert statements.

Manager code does stuff by co-coordinating others.

Manager code is harder to test than worker code because we need to make a choice - do we try to infer its behavior from its outputs using state based testing, or do we use **interaction based testing**?

In interaction based testing, we check that objects talk to each other in the expected fashion. To do this we need to somehow eavesdrop on the conversation. This is achieved by using objects that impersonate real ones.

Usually these are created using a mocking framework.

Mocking Frameworks

Although it is common to refer to all objects created by a mocking framework as mocks this is inaccurate.

A more correct generic term for these objects is *test double*.

These can be subdivided based on how they behave:

- Dummy object - needs to be present to satisfy a type signature but is never actually used
- Stub - must be present and may supply *indirect inputs*
- Mock - verifies that expected interactions take place
- Fake - like a real thing but less heavy - e.g an in memory database
- Spy - object that records its interactions with others

Of these only stubs, mocks and spies might be created by a mocking framework.

We will talk about spies in a moment, but most test doubles can be conceptually viewed as being either a stub or a mock.

The important difference between them is that a mock has an expectation that will cause a test to fail if it is not met. i.e. if an expected method is not called on a mock the test will fail.

A stub does not care if it is called or not - its role is simply to supply values.

Traditional Mocks present a code readability dilemma. They define an expected outcome (a *then*), but are also part of the fixture required for the test to execute (a *given*).

For example with JMock we would write:

```
Mockery context = new Mockery();

// given / arrange
Subscriber subscriber = context.mock(Subscriber.class);
Publisher publisher = new Publisher();
publisher.add(subscriber);

final String message = "message";

// then / assert . . . but we haven't had a when yet
context.checking(new Expectations() {{
  oneOf (subscriber).receive(message);
}});

// when / act
publisher.publish(message);

// then / assert
context.assertIsSatisfied();
```

Spies solve this problem neatly.

Spies

Spies record their interactions with other objects.

In practice this means that Spies act as stubs by default, but as mocks when we want them to.

The given/when/then flow becomes easy and natural to maintain.

For example, using Mockito:

```
// given
Subscriber subscriber = Mockito.mock(Subscriber.class);
Publisher publisher = new Publisher();
publisher.add(subscriber);
String message = "message";

// when
publisher.publish(message);

// then
Mockito.verify(subscriber).receive(message);
```

For this reason we recommend using a spy framework.

When spies act as mocks that must also supply indirect inputs, it is best to make them as forgiving as possible when supplying values but as specific as possible when verifying.

What does this mean?

Lets imagine that, for some reason, the subscribers in our example had to return a positive integer in order for the code to execute without error. Perhaps there is some sort of assert statement in the code:

```
public interface Subscriber {
  int receive(String message);
}
```

We could ensure our test passed as follows:

```
String message = "amessage";
Subscriber subscriber = Mockito.mock(Subscriber.class);
// inject indirect value
Mockito.when(subscriber.receive(message)).thenReturn(1);

Publisher publisher = new Publisher();
publisher.add(subscriber);

publisher.publish(message);

Mockito.verify(subscriber).receive(message);
```

We will not discuss the Mockito API in any detail here, but this line:

```
Mockito.when(subscriber.receive(message)).thenReturn(1);
```

Ensures that when the `receive` method is called on the spy with a string that equals the `message` variable, it will return `1` .

If this line was not present the spy would do what Mockito does by default, which is to return `0` .

What would our test do if, due to a bug, `receive` was called with a different string?

The answer is that, instead of failing due to the verification:

```
Mockito.verify(subscriber).receive(message);
```

It would throw an error before it reached this point because the assertion in our production code would trigger.

We were too specific.

If we instead setup our spy as follows

```
Mockito.when(subscriber.receive(anyString())).thenReturn(1);
```

The test would fail cleanly.

This pattern of being lenient when supplying values, but specific when verifying also tends to result in tests that are less brittle when things change.

Stubs in State-Based Tests

By definition, state-based testing will never include mocks (in the strict sense of the word), but they may use stubs to supply indirect values.

It can be tempting to also use a mocking framework to stub values instead of using their constructors and modifier methods. For complex objects using stubs can appear easier than constructing real ones.

Don't do this.

Mocking frameworks should be used only to isolate our tests from objects with behavior. If you have values that are difficult to construct consider the test data builder pattern instead

Choosing Between State and Interaction Testing

Sometimes there is no choice about which to use. For example, it is not possible to meaningfully specify how a cache should behave from its inputs and outputs alone. Other times we must weigh the pros and cons.

A state-based test for manager code is likely to be less easy to read and understand as it must rely on the behaviors of the objects the SUT interacts with. The test will also be coupled to these behaviors and will require changes if those behaviors change - you have effectively increased the size of the "unit" you are testing as discussed in "Think units not methods".

Interaction-based testing requires us to peek beyond the unit's external interface and into its implementation. This carries the risk that we might over-specify and create an implementation-specific test.

On balance, it is preferable to lean towards state based testing and where possible enable it in the design of your code. There will, however, be many situations in which you will decide that interaction based testing is preferable.

Understand Your Options for Code Reuse

Reusing code is a good thing.

When people start programming in an OO language for the first time they tend to over-use inheritance for this purpose before discovering that composition is generally a better idea.

Unfortunately, it is not easy to use composition to reuse code in JUnit tests and this can lead you to write difficult-to-maintain test class hierarchies.

A small amount of duplication may be preferable to introducing a class hierarchy when other options do not exist, but some types of test can be reused without inheritance.

Assertions

Code related to assertions is straightforward to reuse outside of class hierarchies. This can be done trivially, by creating classes containing static assert methods that can be statically imported (as the built in JUnit assertions now are), or more elegantly by creating custom matchers for hamcrest or AssertJ.

Object Creation

For small, simple objects, the mother pattern can be used, but this can quickly become a maintenance issue if the objects become more complex over time.

A better pattern is the Builder pattern, this can have the added advantage of allowing tests to clearly highlight important and unimportant input.

Repeated Behaviors

If you are using JUnit then repeated section of code within a test can be packaged and re-used as custom rules.

Write Repeatable Unit Tests

Unit tests must be repeatable and deterministic - it must be possible to run them thousands of times in any order and get the same result. This means that they must have no dependency on any external factor.

In practice this means unit tests must not:

- Read or write from databases
- Perform network IO
- Write to disk
- Modify static state

If your test does any of these things then it is not a **unit** test. This is not to say that your test is not valuable.

Only Unit Test Code That It Makes Sense to Unit Test

In most cases, there is little value in unit testing:

- Auto generated code
- Logging
- Code whose **sole** concern is integration with another system

The canonical example of code with a pure integration concern is a DAO.

If a compatible in-memory fake database is available then it can be meaningfully unit tested against that. If no fake is available, there is no value in writing tests that mock out the JDBC driver - the first level of testing should instead be integration testing against a real database.

There is also little value in **explicitly** specifying the behavior of very simple boiler plate code such as get/set methods. The expected behavior is clear without the presence of a test and their actual behavior ought to be verified by other tests that use the code while testing more complex logic. If code coverage indicates that these methods have not been executed by other tests perhaps you can delete them?

Code that is not unit tested should always be integration tested.

Testing FAQ

How Do I Test a Private Method?

You don't test methods (private or public), you test the behavior of a unit as a whole.

If you cannot exercise the logic of a private method via the public interface, is that logic actually required? If it is required, and is sufficiently complex that it is causing you testing pain, then perhaps you should extract that concern into a separate unit that can be tested in isolation and injected in via the constructor?

How Do I Test a Void Method?

You don't test methods (void or not), you test the behavior of a unit as a whole.

If the method is void, it must be performing some sort of side effect that can be checked by either state testing or interaction testing.

For example, if you are trying to 'test the add method' of collection class, you should probably instead be writing tests like:

```
@Test
public void shouldIncreaseInSizeWhenItemsAdded() {
    Collection testee = new ArrayList();
    assertEquals(0, testee.size());
    testee.add("itemA");
    assertEquals(1, testee.size());
    testee.add("itemB");
    assertEquals(2, testee.size());
}
```

How do I Test Code That Reasons About the Current Date/Time?

A bad solution is to use a static method (such as joda time's `setCurrentMillisFixed`) to set the current date.

A good solution is to inject a strategy for retrieving the date/time into your class as a dependency.

Java 8 provides the `java.time.Clock` class which can be used for this purpose.

The static factory method `fixed` will create an instance that represents a constant time. Other methods provide implementations suitable for production use.

Java 7 does not provide an out of the box class for this purpose so you will need to roll your own.

Do I Need to Implement a Teardown Method for my Test?

This used to be a requirement for all JUnit 3 tests. If you didn't nullify all members of a test class in a teardown your test suite began to eat memory as it grew.

This is not a requirement for vanilla JUnit 4 tests, but it is possible that you may need to do so if you are using a custom runner.

What's the Difference Between Errors and Failures?

You should try to design your tests to produce **failures** when the code is logically wrong. Your tests should only produce errors when something unexpected has happened.

How Should I Test for Expected Exceptions?

It depends.

The built in:

```
@Test(expected = FooException.class)
public void shouldThrowFooExceptionWhenFeelsLikeIt
```

Is concise and suffices for simple scenarios, but has a gotcha. If the test method exercises more than one method of the testee, the expectation applies to the whole test method rather than the specific interaction with the testee that is expected to throw it.

If data held within the exception is important, it is also not possible to assert on it with this method.

The traditional solution is to use a try catch block:

```
@Test
public void shouldThrowFooExceptionWhenFeelsLikeIt() {
  try {
    testee.doStuff();
    fail("Expected an exception");
  } catch (FooException expectedException) {
    assertThat(expectedException.getMessage(), is("felt like it"));
  }
}
```

This is easy to follow, but a little verbose. It is also easy to forget to include the call to `fail()` if you are not test driving your code.

JUnit now provides an alternate solution in the form of the 'ExpectedException' method rule. This allows for more fine grained exception checking:

```
@Rule
public ExpectedException thrown= ExpectedException.none();

@Test
public void foo() throws IOException {
  thrown.expect(FooException.class);
  thrown.expectMessage("felt like it");

  testee.doStuff();
}
```

This is more concise, but breaks the usual given/when/then flow of a test by moving the then part to the start of the method.

For Java 8 AssertJ provides some custom assertions that can be used without breaking this flow.

```
@Test
public void testException() {
  assertThatThrownBy(() -> { testee.doStuff(); })
   .isInstanceOf(Exception.class)
   .hasMessageContaining("felt like it");
}
```

Although it maintains the flow, the lambda in which the testee is called looks a little ugly.

When it can be used we recommend sticking with the concise `expected =` format. For more complex situations it is largely a matter of taste.

How Do I Test an Abstract Class?

An abstract class is just a dependency that some other code will use - a dependency that you have made harder than usual to isolate due to your choice to make it an abstract class.

So first off, would your design look better if the functionality was being re-used by composition rather than inheritance?

Assuming that you can't improve your design by getting rid of the abstract class you can either:

- Treat it as an implementation detail and check that each of its clients behaves as expected.
- Test it in isolation by creating an anonymous concrete class

The first approach will result in tests that are less tied to the implementation, but there will be repetition between the tests for each subclass.

The second approach will avoid repetition but is tied to the implementation and is likely to be brittle.

How Do I test Hashcode and Equals?

Testing hashcode and equals can be fiddly and time consuming, which raises questions about whether it is time well spent given that the code is likely to have been auto-generated.

Equals verifier project provides a good (partial) solution:

http://www.jqno.nl/equalsverifier/

It checks that a class fulfills the hashcode-equals contract with a single line test that is trivial to write:

```
@Test
public void shouldObeyHashCodeEqualsContract() {
  EqualsVerifier.forClass(MyValue.class).verify();
}
```

It does, however, do a very thorough job of checking the contract - including how it interacts with inheritance. It is non-trivial to make a non-final class conform to the contract.

Although equals verifier does a good job of checking the hashcode equals contract, it has no knowledge of how you expect the methods to actually behave. If you wish equality to (for example) be defined by a single ID field only, you must write additional tests that verify this behavior.

For the common scenario of a class that should be considered equal based on all of its fields the behavior may be checked in a single test:

```
@Test
public void shouldObeyHashCodeEqualsContract() {
  EqualsVerifier.forClass(MyValue.class).allFieldsShouldBeUsed().verify();
}
```

This may become the default behavior in a future version of EqualsVerifier, but must be specifically specified in 1.7.5

Bad Advice

Some truly terrible ideas are commonly circulated as "best practice". In this section we provide examples and explain why they should be ignored.

Bad Advice - Single Exit Point Rules

Some coding standards mandate that all methods should have a single exit point.

Doing so can be damaging, particularly when it is enforced by static analysis.

Details

Single exit point is an idea with a long history dating back to the era of liberally applied gotos and spaghetti code.

In that context, adding constraints on what could happen within a function was helpful. Knowing that there is only one point that a large function can exit from makes it easier to understand.

Many modern functional languages continue to either enforce or encourage single exit points.

So it must be a good idea to add this constraint to Java right?

Lets look what happens when we are told we must only have one exit point:

Single exit with statements

```
public class Example {
  private int value;

  public int single(int x) {
    int retVal = 0;

    if (x == 10) {
      retVal = -value;
    } else if (x > 0) {
      retVal = value + x;
    }

    return retVal;
  }

}
```

If we remove the single exit point constraint we get:

Multiple exit

```
public class Example {
  private int value;

  public int multi(int x) {
    if (x == 10) {
      return -value;
    }

    if (x > 0) {
      return value + x;
    }

    return 0;
  }
}
```

Which version is better?

There isn't much in it, but the multiple exit point version is easier to comprehend.

Trying to apply the single exit point constraint resulted in an additional local variable to hold return state. In the multi exit version we can clearly see what is returned when none of the conditions match. In the single exit version it is slightly less clear as the returned value is declared at the start of the method then overwritten.

So does this mean that single exit point methods are bad?

No.

It is possible to write alternate single exit implementations.

```
  public int oneAssignment(int x) {
    final int retVal;

    if (x == 10) {
      retVal = -value;
    } else if (x > 0) {
      retVal = value + x;
    } else {
      retVal = 0;
    }

    return retVal;
  }
```

We've addressed the issues we identified earlier. We only assign to `retVal` once and it is clear what is assigned when none of the conditions match.

Is this superior in some way to the multi exit version?

Not really.

We can also write a single exit method using the `?` operator:

Single exit with the ? operator

```
public int expression(int x) {
  return  x ==  10 ? -value
      : x > 0  ? value + x
      : 0;
}
```

We have switched from using a statement (if) to working with expressions (i.e. things that return a value). This allows us to get rid of the additional variable while maintaining a single exit point.

Is this version clearer than the multi-exit version? That is debatable and ultimately a matter of personal taste.

The code using `?` is terse and some will find it harder to understand.

The multi-exit version is more verbose but its proponents would argue it is easier to comprehend.

If your personal preference is for the `?` operator version, it still does not follow that the single exit point rule is something you should try to universally apply.

The most likely result is that you will push people towards writing code like the earlier bloated version of our method. As Java is a largely statement-based language, you will also encounter logic where the multi-exit version is undeniably clearer.

Martin Fowler and Kent Beck express things nicely in "Refactoring: Improving the Design of Existing Code"

> ". . . one exit point is really not a useful rule. Clarity is the key principle: If the method is clearer with one exit point, use one exit point; otherwise don't"

There is nothing wrong with single exit functions, but only write them when it makes sense to do so.

Bad Advice - Always Use a StringBuffer to Concatenate

This advice is doubly wrong.

Firstly it advocates using the synchronized `StringBuffer` rather than a `StringBuilder` .

Secondly it is an oversimplification or misunderstanding of the more nuanced and reasonable advice to not concatenate Strings in a loop.

Avoiding concatenation in a loop is reasonable. Using a `StringBuilder` is likely to be more efficient if the loop executes a reasonable number of times as it will avoid string allocations.

The performance difference is unlikely to be significant in most cases, but the resulting code isn't noticeably less-readable - so it is a premature optimization without a cost.

Lets see what happens when we apply this advice when no loop is present:

```
public String buffer(String s, int i) {
  StringBuilder sb = new StringBuilder();
  sb.append("Foo");
  sb.append(s);
  sb.append(i);
  return sb.toString();
}

public String concat(String s, int i) {
  return "Foo" + s + i;
}
```

The `concat` version is far clearer.

Is it less efficient?

The eclipse compiler generates the following bytecode for `concat` :

```
NEW java/lang/StringBuilder
DUP
LDC "Foo"
INVOKESPECIAL java/lang/StringBuilder.<init> (Ljava/lang/String;)V
ALOAD 1
INVOKEVIRTUAL java/lang/StringBuilder.append /
   (Ljava/lang/String;)Ljava/lang/StringBuilder;
ILOAD 2
INVOKEVIRTUAL java/lang/StringBuilder.append (I)Ljava/lang/StringBuilder;
INVOKEVIRTUAL java/lang/StringBuilder.toString ()Ljava/lang/String;
ARETURN
```

A `StringBuilder` is created by the compiler behind the scenes to handle the concatenation so our simpler cleaner code produces identical bytecode to the more verbose option.

The presence of loops in the code may prevent the compiler performing this optimization, but code without branches will be optimized every time. Although compilers may exist that do not support this optimization it is unlikely that you will ever use them.

Bad Advice - Hungarian Notation

The idea of Hungarian notation and similar schemes is to reflect the type, scope or other attribute of a variable in its name.

For example:

- bFlag
- nSize
- m_nSize

Where `b` indicates a Boolean type, `n` an integer type and `m_` that the named variable is a field.

This is a terrible idea.

Such notation *might* be useful if you are reading code printed to paper, but all the information it provides is readily available in a modern IDE.

Naming things is hard enough without adding additional concerns that the name must handle.

These types of notation are like comments. They add noise and must be maintained in tandem with the information they duplicate. If extra effort is not spent to maintain them they become misleading.

Uncle Bob Martin puts it nicely:

> "nowadays, HN and other forms of type encoding are simply impediments. They make it harder to change the name or type of a variable, function, member or class. They make it harder to read the code. And they create the possibility that the encoding system will mislead the reader"

www.ingramcontent.com/pod-product-compliance
Lightning Source LLC
LaVergne TN
LVHW082127070326
832902LV00040B/2926
* 9 7 8 9 8 8 8 4 0 7 2 1 7 *